MW01505071

HILTON CARTER
UNFURLED

HILTON CARTER

UNFURLED

Designing a living home

CICO BOOKS

This book is dedicated to Holland, Vada and Fiona—my heart, my home.

Photographer and stylist Hilton Carter
Senior designer Megan Smith
Senior commissioning editor
   Annabel Morgan
Creative director Leslie Harrington
Head of production
   Patricia Harrington

Published in 2025 by CICO Books
An imprint of Ryland Peters & Small
Ltd
20–21 Jockey's Fields
London WC1R 4BW
and 1452 Davis Bugg Road
Warrenton, NC 27579, USA
www.rylandpeters.com

10 9 8 7 6 5 4 3 2 1

Text © Hilton Carter 2025
Design and photography
© CICO Books 2025

The author's moral rights have
been asserted. All rights reserved.
No part of this publication may be
reproduced, stored in a retrieval
system, or transmitted in any form
or by any means, electronic,
mechanical, photocopying, or
otherwise, without the prior
permission of the publisher.

A CIP catalog record for this book is
available from the Library of Congress
and the British Library.

ISBN: 978-1-80065-572-0

Printed in Slovenia

MIX
Paper | Supporting
responsible forestry
FSC® C106600

ROOM ASPECT AND LIGHT LEVELS
Understanding the types of light you
have in your home is essential when
choosing the right plants for each
space. Here's a breakdown of the
types of natural light your plants
will typically receive if you live in
the northern hemisphere like I do,
depending on the direction in which
a window is facing. (Note that these
directions will be reversed if you live
in the southern hemisphere)

NORTH-FACING ASPECT Receives low
to medium indirect light
EAST-FACING ASPECT Receives direct
morning sunlight to bright indirect
light
SOUTH-FACING ASPECT Receives
bright indirect light for most of the day
WEST-FACING ASPECT Receives
bright indirect light to direct afternoon
sunlight

Contents

A Home Unfurled   6

Home Lush Home   14

The Exterior   16

The Entryway   24

The Living Room   32

Designing lighting   *46*

The Kitchen   50

Styling floating shelves   *66*

The Dining Room   68

The Powder Room   80

The Sunroom   88

Styling a coffee table   *104*

Second Time Around   106

The Suite Entry   108

The Primary Bedroom   110

Designing a Gallery Wall   *124*

The Bathroom   128

The Dressing Room   140

The Toddler Room   150

The Nursery   162

The Guest Room   172

Floor Decor   *186*

The Studio   188

Last Thoughts   202

Credits   205

Index   206

Thanks   208

A HOME
UNFURLED

I want to tell you a story about interior styling and design. I hate to admit this, but when I was younger, I didn't know that styling a room was called interior design. I actually thought it was called—wait a minute, what's that face you're making? OK, I know what you're thinking. "This book isn't about plants?" But I hope that thought brings a smile of excitement to your face rather than a frown of disappointment. I get it. I've always dreamed of creating an interiors book, but I never imagined I'd have the chance to make one that wasn't focused on plants. Listen, I never thought I would have the opportunity to write and photograph one book about plants, let alone five. But here we are.

While you're seeing the interior stylist Hilton Carter in this book for the first time, this has been my reality for a while. You see, over the past ten years I've leaned into the idea of living a full life. One that is nurtured by the people and possibilities I seek out and which has unfurled slowly, like a poppy. You may have only one life, but you are not defined by just one thing. So while many might know me as the "plant guy," others know me as the "film guy," and some, from many years ago, as the "painter." The truth is that we are never just one thing. Each of us has the ability to create and become whatever we dedicate our minds, hearts, and energy to. That might sound a little "woo woo," but I know it to be true because that's what happened to me.

From the age of four, I wanted to be an artist. I remember once crying to my mother when I couldn't think of something to draw. When she tried to console me by suggesting I trace something, the mere suggestion sparked rage in my little four-year-old heart. "I am an artist, and artists don't trace!" There was a fire in me driving me to create.

My passion led me to attend a magnet high school specializing in art, which paved the way for a Bachelor of Fine Arts degree in college. Before leaving Maryland Institute College of Art (MICA), I started to feel the draw of filmmaking.

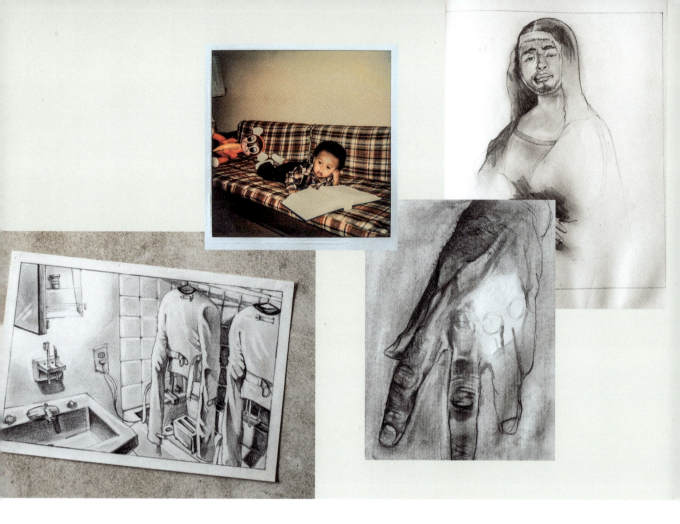

As a painter, my work was mainly figurative, telling a story with each piece. But I began to realize how limiting a single frame was for conveying a narrative. It wasn't that way for filmmakers. They could take their audience through all the emotions, from beginning to middle to end. I loved that. And I loved movies. So after graduating from MICA, I moved to Los Angeles to attend graduate school for film.

It was here that I learned to participate in every aspect of filmmaking. Unlike painting, where you work alone, a filmmaker collaborates with other creatives to make a single piece of art. To become a director, I first had to master editing, acting, sound design, cinematography, and—most importantly—production design, which was the one that changed everything for me. In production design, everything comes down to the details. Everything you add to a space tells a story about the individuals who live in that space, without them even appearing on screen. I started to reflect on my own space and what it revealed about me. And that's when I decided to "production design" my own home. Oh yeah, that's what I was trying to say before you interrupted me with that look of surprise. That's right—I thought when you designed or styled a space, you were "production designing" it.

I worked as a freelance filmmaker until ten years ago, when I was offered a job at an advertising agency. As a freelance artist, I had no idea what terms like PTO or 401(k) meant, but they sounded pretty good. You can live differently when you don't have to worry about where your next paycheck is coming from. But it's not as free as working for yourself, and I missed that freedom. After a year at the ad agency, I decided to start a side hustle in interior styling rooms, and this was when Fiona, then my girlfriend and now my wife, suggested I post images of our apartment on social media as it could lead to other opportunities. I took her advice

and started posting on Instagram. But although my intention was to show off my interior styling, more and more people started to comment on the plant styling in our home. In 2019 my first book, *Wild at Home*, was published and I left my job. And while so many have enjoyed the ways that I've styled and nurtured plants in spaces all across the country, it's the spaces that I've interior styled that truly bring everything to life for me.

When Fiona and I purchased our home in 2020, I had the opportunity to create a living space for my family. And with this opportunity came the knowledge that making something beautiful doesn't

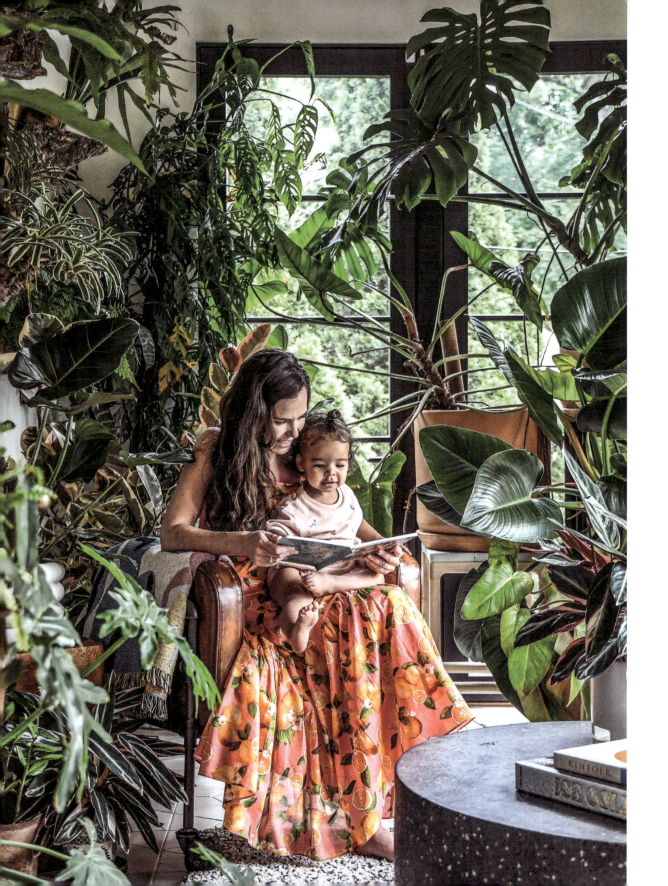

happen overnight. Creating a home takes time. It can be slow and requires a lot of patience, planning, deliberation, and intentional decision-making. But eventually, given love and thought and care, that home will unfurl to reveal its true beauty.

We chose this home because we were ready to start a family, so when the time came to design and style it, I thought about how family life might evolve over time. That vision has guided many of my decisions, because, for me, the first step in designing a living home is to ensure that the choices made are practical ones, rooted in everyday life. The second step focuses on aesthetics. Before working on our home, I had never analyzed my signature style but now I'd define it as "modern lush." It's a combination of modern design styles with a strong emphasis on simplicity, functionality, and clean lines. Sleek forms are combined with organic shapes and abundant greenery unfurling all around. The advice I'd give to someone trying to find their own style is to lean toward what comes naturally. It should be something you feel instinctively connected to, not a box you're trying to fit yourself into. I have always loved being surrounded by plants and blurring the line between being indoors and out, and in an interior, I will always find a place for greenery to add life and color.

My starting point when it comes to styling a space is the feeling I want that room to evoke. Once I've defined that feeling, I think about the colors that spark the same emotion and build a moodboard around that palette. This guides my design decisions about the colors, textures, shapes, and scale of the pieces in the room. I'm not afraid

to admit that I design with my heart on my sleeve, seeking a balance between form and function and the emotional thread that ties a space together.

Just like us, our home is a work in progress. And as time passes, it will develop and evolve to meet our changing needs. The day Fiona and I moved in was the day a seed was planted. Since then, we have been nurturing it, watching the seed sprout and climb, put out branches and leaves and buds. Those buds started to unfurl and are still unfurling now. And while it may be years before our home is in full bloom, the plan is to enjoy every single moment of the process, because it is so precious, delicate, and fleeting.

HOME LUSH HOME

There are few things in life as sweet as tasting the fruits of your own labor. Fiona and I dreamed of one day having a home together and this is our dream realized. What you're seeing here is the result of much time, money, effort, and, of course, love. Our home didn't start out this way and I'm going to take you through the journey—the discussions, decisions, headaches, and achievements—that brought it to where it is today. The process has taken place over two separate renovations so far, beginning with the exterior and the first floor of the home. So that's where we'll start. As someone who loves being surrounded by greenery, living in a home that radiates lushness from the street instantly captured our hearts and became everything we wanted.

The exterior

The day you consider purchasing your first home is a special day, but the day you know you've found the home of your dreams, your "forever home," is a day you'll never forget. I know this because for Fiona and me, it feels as if it was yesterday. It was 2020 and we were in the midst of the Coronavirus pandemic. At the time, we were living in an apartment and life felt so uncertain. We had made an offer on another home earlier in the year, before the pandemic hit, but once everything shut down that March, we decided to pull out of the deal. This wasn't a decision we made lightly and we were anxious we wouldn't find anything else that we loved or even liked. However, at that moment, my work was on pause and Fiona, who is a dentist and has her own practice, had to close her doors.

A few months passed, life seemed to open up again, and we felt comfortable looking at houses. On a warm evening in July 2020, we decided to view our future home on a whim because it was close to Fiona's dental practice and if we're anything, we're a family that believes in convenience. I mean, Fiona and I originally met because we were next-door neighbors, but that's a story for another time.

The house had been on the market for a while and beyond the fact that we were deep in a pandemic, the only other reasons I can think it hadn't sold were that it wasn't easily viewable from the road and the online images of the home didn't show the true charm of the interior and the incredible silhouette of the façade. When we pulled up on the driveway, it was early evening, and the sun and clouds were collaborating to create the most magical sunset. Between the trees I saw the front of the house and I was transfixed.

I can't say that it was exactly love at first sight, but I could see the potential right there in front of my eyes. Now the house did have some cosmetic issues. The mixed flagstone entry terrace hadn't been maintained in a while and was covered in moss and algae. The stucco facade was patchy and peeling. We liked the windows, but while they looked pretty from a distance, close up some of them were inoperable or broken. Book-ending many of them were shutters which, in a few cases, like the ones on the sides of the living-room window, served no purpose. The front yard was pleasant but many of the shrubs were sparse or dying back. The one plant that helped woo us was the sweet bay magnolia, or *Magnolia virginiana*, directly in front of the house. While the house had a great silhouette, many changes would be necessary to restore its glow.

Concept and moodboard

When considering the look of the home from the outside, I appreciated the vibe that already existed. After all, it was the front of the house that pulled me in when we first saw it. The color palette was fine, but I wanted to turn the original colors from cool to warm, so the house felt welcoming and cared for. I decided to repaint the facade in a warm white (Greek Villa) and refresh the shutters, gable end, and front door with a brighter, warmer green (Basil) for a subtle lift. For the windows, I chose black frames to add a modern touch to the home's timeless style.

When it came to planning the garden, the idea was simple—make it lush. In keeping with the style of the house, boxwoods and topiary trees felt like ideal partners for the sweet bay magnolia. We added more mixed flagstone and, at the back of the house, a deck of warm-toned wood. The thing we both knew the moment we laid eyes on the house was that it had a vibe, and our job was to enhance this.

THE BLANK CANVAS
This is the view that greeted us on the day we first drove up to the house. We were instantly pulled in by its charming silhouette and the lush greenery of the garden.

MY CHOSEN PALETTE

» The stucco is Sherwin-Williams 7551 Greek Villa and the gable end, doors, and shutters Sherwin-Williams 6194 Basil.

» New boxwoods surround the existing sweet bay magnolia. In summer, I style my tropical plants on the entry terrace.

» The old wooden window frames were replaced with black metal and we replaced the concrete path with new flagstone.

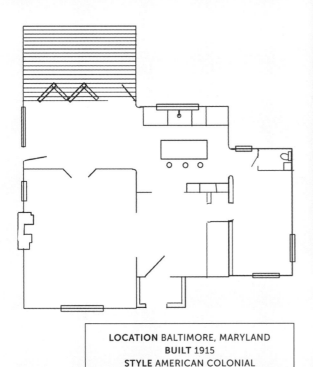

LOCATION BALTIMORE, MARYLAND
BUILT 1915
STYLE AMERICAN COLONIAL
SQUARE FOOTAGE 3,600 SQ FT/335 SQ M
BEDROOMS 4 (5 BEFORE RENOVATION)
BATHROOMS 2.5

Plan and layout

Many old, established neighborhoods like ours have a homeowners' association that enforces the principle of keeping all the homes in the community looking as they did when first built. If you want to make alterations to the exterior of the home, you must submit a request, detailing your list of changes, and hope that those on the board will approve them. When we began house-hunting around Baltimore, neighborhoods with strict regulations on what could be done to the homes made it difficult for us to find our dream house. Luckily, in what has become our neighborhood, the rules weren't as inflexible and mainly focused on the front and sides of the house. This meant the exterior paint color would have to stay close to the original, and any existing shutters would need to remain in situ.

The shutters on the living-room window didn't fully cover the window when closed, so we requested permission to have them removed. The biggest ask that we put to the board was to replace all the windows with modern, black-framed ones, while adding a window to the front of the house and accordion-style doors at the rear, plus a raised deck. To improve our chances of selling this idea to the board, we hired architect Mark Mobley to design the windows. We went with Andersen Windows because of their ability to make any idea you have come to life. Mark drew up the images for the new windows, and added our request for the new paint colors and the deck. We submitted our request to the board and, after a week or so of crossed fingers and toes, received their approval. Now work could begin.

HOME GROWN

We knew we'd need to make a few cosmetic changes to the exterior of the house but wanted to keep its original shine (top). With new windows, fresh paint, and more greenery, you can really see the difference. Plans for the new windows (above).

Knowing our limits, we hired professionals to do the building, the millwork, the general contracting, and project management. After considering a few options, the company we used was Guerrilla Construction. When they started work, it was so stressful to see a "move-in ready" home get torn apart, but what was to come would change our home and the way we live in it forever.

I'm aware of the debate about removing old windows—in my opinion, if it's necessary and you have it in the budget, do what's best for your home. It's possible to donate old windows or utilize them in imaginative ways, like building a greenhouse. We had a large number of windows that needed to be replaced, so to make sure the look was consistent throughout, we decided to replace all of them. The new windows have transformed the appearance of the house, giving it a new youthful look, plus the light they let into the home is life itself!

Once the new windows were in, the patching of the stucco finish was carried out. There were just a few spots on the back of the house that needed to be fixed, but it's a process-heavy job. After that we had the entire house—from the doors and shutters to the gable end—painted.

All it took for the flagstone on the entry terrace to look brand-new was a quick power wash. And if you've ever power washed something, you know the joy and satisfaction it brings. There's something magical about watching years of grime blasted away in moments. When we purchased the house, we had no idea what the true color of the flagstone actually was, but once it was power washed, we were floored by the vibrant hues, variations, and sparkle. The issue with the flagstone was that it was only on the entry terrace and not along the entire walkway, so we called on Turner Landscaping to redo this using mixed flagstone, so that it would feel connected to the terrace.

As Turner were on site, we had them help with the landscaping as well. They removed everything except the magnolia and a laurel and used *Buxus microphylla* 'Little Missy' to create planting beds at

BACKYARD BLISS
The back of the house felt a little unloved and unattractive to us when we viewed the home (above left). Our exterior architect Mark Mobley sketched out the plan for the new exterior look of the house (above right). The back would now have a deck and new windows—real bliss (opposite).

the front of the house. Here we planted Japanese painted fern (*Athyrium niponicum* var. *pictum*), cinnamon fern (*Osmunda cinnamomea*), *Allium* 'Ambassador', *Ligularia dentata* 'Desdemona', a Japanese maple, and a pom-pom juniper. In winter, many of the plants lose their leaves, but from spring through fall, the greenery here is spectacular. During the warmer months, I add a little extra icing to the cake by styling some of my indoor plants on the entry terrace to make the space feel tropical and lush. The large spindle palm (*Hyophorbe verschaffeltii*), Swiss cheese plant (*Monstera deliciosa),* and *Philodendron* 'Congo' grow wild during their "summer break" and give our house a Southern California look right here in Baltimore.

TOP 5 IMPACTFUL ADDITIONS TO ENHANCE THE FRONT OF YOUR HOME

Statement plants! You knew I was going to start there. You can quickly make your home feel more expensive by adding cool, manicured plants. Pro-tip: adding symmetry around the front door can be boring and predictable, so make sure you're creating that unexpected "wow" moment.

Paint the front door a bright, bold color. It's a quick and inexpensive way to give the facade of your home a fresh focal point.

Power wash it. Over time everything gets a little grimy and mucky out in the elements. Power washing brings the life back to whatever you're working on.

Lighting. This is one of the things that's often forgotten, but having great sconces or garden lighting really makes a home stand out and feel good to come home to.

Stylish seating. Seating and tables provide a welcoming atmosphere. Give yourself a small area to enjoy a cup of coffee while doomscrolling on your phone.

The entryway

There are few things in life that you get a second chance at, and a first impression isn't one of them. When you enter a home, the entryway needs to strike exactly the right welcoming note. On the day we came to view our house, I remember being so impressed that the front door didn't open straight into the living room. Growing up in apartments, there was no such thing as an entryway, let alone a foyer. The entryway here was quaint and gracious–just what we were hoping for. This isn't a part of the home where you're going to spend a great deal of time, but it provides an important backdrop for hellos and goodbyes. It's the opening moment. It sets the scene and provides a small vignette of what your design style is all about. We didn't have much space here, but I wanted to make what we did have impactful.

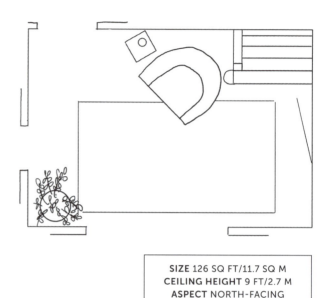

SIZE 126 SQ FT/11.7 SQ M
CEILING HEIGHT 9 FT/2.7 M
ASPECT NORTH-FACING

Concept and moodboard

The entryway should be somewhere that features the colors and textures present in other main rooms in the house, giving an idea of what is to come and leading harmoniously into other spaces. When it came to creating a moodboard for this space, I waited until we had decided exactly what we were doing in the living room and kitchen, given that these two rooms lead off the entryway, which needed to play a supporting role to those two stars.

Once I had developed moodboards for the kitchen and living room, I knew colors like white and gray would complement the kitchen design, with stronger colors like red and black complementing the living-room decor. Various different types of wood would be prevalent throughout the house, with touches of rattan here and there, so I wanted to bring in these textures too. Overall, my vision was for a space that felt uncluttered, bright, and welcoming.

Plan and layout

There are many interesting ways that you could go about styling an entryway, but first and foremost the welcome it extends should always feel special. However, my first impression of our entryway was that it felt dark and a little gloomy, a situation that was not helped by the dated wallpaper. This space is north-facing, and the only window was the glazed panel in the front door, which itself is set under a covered entry, so there wasn't much natural light making its way into the room. As a result, we made two changes to the entryway when we renovated.

THE BLANK CANVAS
This image shows how dark and gloomy the stairway was before we renovated (above left). The staircase connects the house and should feel lively and welcoming. Even though it wasn't what we wanted at first, the space was very workable.

SW 7028
Incredible White

MY CHOSEN PALETTE

» Once the adjoining rooms on this floor were styled, I took inspiration from them for the entryway palette.

» During the first round of renovations we painted all the walls with Sherwin-Williams 7028 Incredible White and the ceilings in 7007 Ceiling Bright White.

» Textures like brass, rattan, red oak, linen, and greenery all complement the reds in the painting by Emma Childs.

Furniture

The next stage was the furniture. As mentioned, we remove our outdoor shoes when entering the house, so I needed to find the right spot for taking off and putting on shoes. While the space didn't lend itself to storage for multiple pairs of shoes and coats, some sort of chair or bench was required, and I went with a generous rattan chair that could comfortably hold many different sizes of people. While the entryway isn't somewhere for extended hangouts, I wanted to make sure the chair would encourage visitors to take the load off, if they felt so inclined. Having said that, I have to confess that, while the chair does get a lot of use, we tend to perch on the bottom stairs of the staircase while changing our shoes, as do many of our guests. It reminds me of when you purchase a new toy for your cat, and they ignore the toy in favor of the box it came in.

Next to the chair I styled a small wooden end table that I found in a thrift store during my time in New Orleans. This has bounced around with me from apartment to apartment and found its way here to create this perfect moment. On top, a small modern table lamp radiates a warm glow of light as you enter. With its opaque shade, it diffuses the light enough not to become too overbearing. On the topic of lighting, on the ceiling above, I hung an hourglass-shaped pendant light. Its black matte exterior picks up on the color of the window frames and other pieces in the living room, while the gold interior hints at the many gold accents scattered throughout the first floor.

Since the room is mainly a connecting space, the center remains wide open, with the walls and corners bringing all the fun. On the wall between the entryway and dining room, I mounted a small antique brass coat rack. To the left of that hangs a painting by artist Emma Childs that adds a wonderful pop of red, balancing that of the rug.

One was the removal of the old-fashioned wallpaper and the other, bigger change was the addition of a new window part way up the staircase, in order to bring more light into this space.

With these two alterations made, I was ready to get started on furnishing and decorating the space. This area would be where we took off or put on our shoes and coats when entering and exiting the house, so it needed to be practical as well as inviting. So I started with the perfect rug, given that this would be the first thing you saw as the door swung open and also necessary as we are a "shoe-off" household. A Persian rug exudes a sense of timeless elegance and I sourced a rich pomegranate-red Persian with a mix of colors that would reappear throughout the house (see pages 186–187 for more on Floor Decor).

COZY CORNERS

Placing this window by the staircase brought so much light and life to the entry (opposite). A ZZ plant is styled in a black metal planter below a framed copy of *Vanity Fair* Italy, where an image of my old apartment made the cover (right). I styled a wicker chair at the foot of the stairs which serves as a comfortable place to sit and take off our shoes, or another place for our cat Pepper to lounge (below).

On the other side of the room is a framed copy of Italian *Vanity Fair*, with one of my photographs of our old apartment gracing the cover. Below that, in a sleek matte black planter, I styled a ZZ plant (*Zamioculcas zamiifolia*). I've mentioned the lack of light in this area, and the ZZ plant understands just how to adapt to lower light levels.

VIBRANT VIEWS
Abstract painter Emma Childs' colorful work hangs in the entryway, echoing the red and warm tones throughout our first floor. As you enter the home, the kitchen is directly in view and Emma's painting lures you to come closer.

Speaking of plants, halfway up the stairs, I styled a vigorous snake plant (*Dracaena trifasciata* subsp. *trifasciata*) in front of a mirror—because what entryway would be complete without a mirror? I placed a tall, floor-length one here, not only so we can check our attire before we exit the house but also because it changed the feel and mood of the staircase for the better. Positioning the mirror means the light from the new window is doubled and reflected right back into the middle of the entryway.

The design of this room provides a warm welcome for our family as well as those who we are fortunate enough to have come visit us. It also sets the scene for the decorative themes to come on the first floor, creating a sense of cohesion.

TOP 5 ENTRYWAY MUST-HAVES

A stylish mirror This allows you to check on your look before you leave the house and helps to reflect light back into the room. However, don't have a mirror face the front door. That's just bad design.

A statement rug The first thing you and your guests make contact with on entering the house, rugs help center an entryway and set the vibe of the room. If you have a "shoes-off" household, a shag or Berber rug feels great under your feet.

A stylish catch-all bowl or tray If you're like me, you need a designated place to put your keys or wallet, so that you're not searching the house for them right when you need to leave. A bowl or tray can be placed on an end table or bench, or mounted on the wall.

Storage baskets Baskets fit neatly in corners or beneath a bench. Ones with lids are a plus as they hide mess and clutter away.

A shoe horn As you mature, there are many things you start to realize are necessary in life. A shoe horn might not seem like a major must-have but you'll find it just makes your mornings run more smoothly.

The living room

Did you know the living room is one of the few rooms that adds to your home's curb appeal? From the street, your living room can give your neighbors a peek into your home and a glimpse of the life that goes on behind its exterior. I once relocated from Venice, California, to New Orleans, purely because on a visit to New Orleans, I saw into the living room of one home and, in that moment, fell in love with the city. I could feel the room, or rather the city, calling me, inviting me to become part of its history. I learned then that a living room should tell the story of those who live in the space, just as a shop window entices customers and showcases a brand's identity.

A living room should make you feel comfortable and relaxed, right? Well, the living room in the house that I grew up in, and shared with my grandmother, mother, aunt, and uncle, was the complete opposite. In fact, it had the appearance of a kill room. Who remembers the TV crime drama *Dexter*? The main character was a serial killer who would fully wrap a room in plastic before killing his prey. And this was exactly the case with my grandmother's living room. Everything was covered in plastic. To be fully transparent—rather like the plastic covers that wrapped the furniture—the living room was not there to be lived in. Far from it. The only people who were allowed to sit in there were special guests or family coming in from out of town. And even they had to struggle to get comfortable on those hot, sticky, slippery plastic coverings. It was here, as a kid, that I promised myself, that when I had my own home, every single room in it would be lived in and enjoyed. And so when it came to designing our living room, a truly living and lived-in space was my goal.

Concept and moodboard

When it came to putting together the moodboard for this room, we went for white walls, relying on the decor to introduce moodier, darker notes that would bring the space an organic, grounded, and soulful feel. I put together a color palette featuring earthy neutrals, greens, dark grays, and warm woods that make the space feel cozy, while pops of strong color, including deep reds, amber, and ocher, add depth and vibrancy. Texture is high on my list of essentials when styling an inviting living space, and here I wanted to introduce natural textures like raw woods, woven textiles, and intricate stonework to provide tactile warmth.

THE BLANK CANVAS

Images of our living room before the renovation (above). The space had lots of potential for redesigning and being opened up, which is what we did while keeping the original features we loved, like the fireplace and the French doors into the sunroom. The new living room has stayed pretty close to the original layout aside from a few upgrades like wall color and windows.

MY CHOSEN PALETTE

» When styling the living room, it's all about creating a warm and calming atmosphere.

» With the walls painted with Sherwin Williams 7028 Incredible White and the ceilings in 7007 Ceiling Bright White to brighten the overall space, I used colors from the decor and artwork to make the room feel rich and welcoming.

» The colors in the agate stone coffee table pull together the natural elements in the room.

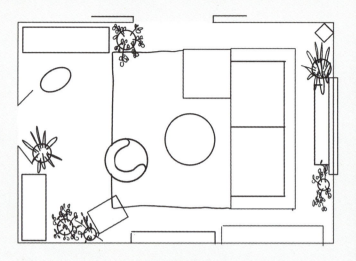

SIZE 210 SQ FT/19.5 SQ M
CEILING HEIGHT 9 FT/2.7 M
ASPECT NORTH- & EAST-FACING

Plan and layout

The plan for the living room was simple because it presented itself to us that way. When we first walked into the house, we couldn't see anything here that needed renovating. But please note the operative word: "see." We had the house inspected before purchase and were aware of many issues that the inspector uncovered. But it wasn't until the contractors started removing walls to replace the outdated electrical wiring that they discovered inactive termite damage under the flooring in the living room.

We could have addressed this problem in a few different ways. The most budget-friendly approach would have been to remove the damaged areas and replace them with new flooring, matching it to the original wooden flooring as closely as possible. As that would create a lot of uncertainty as to the end result, we decided to replace the entire living-room floor. However, we were also planning to swap around the existing kitchen and dining room, so the flooring in the old kitchen also needed replacing. And if the flooring in the living room was going to be new, and the flooring in the new dining room was going to be new, the only

BRIGHT AND BOLD
The beauty of creating layers of color and texture (above). Looking from the living room into the entryway and dining room, you can see how decisions made for one room play a role in decisions for others. Each room is its own chapter; together they create a story.

areas with the original wood floors would have been the kitchen and the entryway. Eventually, in order to avoid the first floor having two different types of flooring, and to make everything feel and look consistent, we decided to fit all-new flooring throughout the first floor.

We didn't make this decision lightly, because I can't even express to you how hard it was watching the contractor and his team rip up the original flooring. The flooring was one of the reasons we fell in love with the house. It was heartbreaking, but we decided to replace it with something that was close

STYLE TIP

When it comes to creating the right vibe for your living room, start with finding the perfect rug. This should ideally cover most of the floor, set the right tone, and anchor the room. A rug's shape, pattern, and texture can also play a key role in guiding the selection and placement of furniture in a room.

to what was there before, just brand-new. We chose red oak because not only did it pretty much match the original flooring throughout the rest of the house, but it's also a hardwood and can stand up to a lot of punishment. Listen, if you have pets or you're someone who parties with individuals that like to wear high heels, take a tip from me and make sure the flooring in your home is made from a hardwood. We chose Ipswich Pine stain for its warmth and depth and went with a semi-gloss finish to match the flooring elsewhere.

Once the new floor had been laid, not much else needed to change. One thing we were set on was retaining the charming details that the house possessed. For instance, we kept the French doors that lead from the living room into the sunroom. These doors not only have an old-school charm but also allow us to close off one area from the other when needed. In many of the rooms that weren't fully renovated, like this one, we kept the picture rail just below the ceiling. Most American Colonials have this feature, which reminds me of the homes I saw in New Orleans. We added a few recessed ceiling lights, gave the walls a fresh coat of white paint and the fireplace a new coat of black, and then it was time to style the room.

LEVELS

Our Cloud Couch sits just below the bookshelf, giving us a good reason to relax while reading a book (opposite). But when styling the room, it was about creating levels that would move the eye from the floor to the ceiling. Levels of texture and light (above). Finding creative ways to place lighting throughout a room makes the space feel more dramatic and intimate. Utilizing the top of the armoire brings energy and life higher into the room.

Furniture

A fireplace can be one of the finest features in a room, but the discussion around what to hang above it has tested relationships since the dawn of time. The debate about whether it should be a television or a piece of art can become heated. I decided to split the difference, so that we could have our cake and eat it too. We hung a Frame TV over the fireplace, so when we're in the mood to put our feet up and lounge we can watch the TV, but if the room is hosting a more formal gathering, we can have it display a work of art. As I don't like to see wiring sticking out, we built the wall out a bit so that we could conceal the TV wires in the wall.

On the wall next to the fireplace, I placed twin white metal bookcases with cabinets below. Their minimalistic design blends perfectly with the lines of the room, and the pristine white makes them almost look built into the wall. Against all this white, the book spines create a pop of color. The cabinets below are great for storing additional dinnerware and, of course, kids' toys and books. When you have small children, one way to make sure they don't take over your living room is to have plenty of storage to hide their things. By the French doors to the sunroom, I placed a tall black armoire with rattan doors and drawers. Its height makes it perfect for storing items like glassware and barware, and it's tall enough to store a wicker basket for toys beneath.

In the center of the room, I rolled out a large blush hand-tufted wool rug with a quiet striped pattern that grounds the room. If the rug is quiet, the round green agate coffee table is loud. While the agate is unpredictable in its varying hues, the table's acacia wood legs strike the perfect balance between the bold agate top and the wool rug below. The main feature here is the Cloud Couch from RH, described as "the most comfortable" couch because it is just that. They say bigger is better, and it is large.

I describe it as "boneless", because it feels just like a big cushy pillow. I went with a textured linen fabric in a gray color named Fog, because you can never go wrong with linen and the color plays well with the grays we've utilized in other rooms. If you have pets or children, it's smart to use darker fabrics for your couch, to hide the inevitable stains and blemishes—and I say this from painful experience.

On the other side of the coffee table, facing the couch, is a charcoal gray-upholstered swivel chair, because everyone needs an accent chair that allows them to spin 360 degrees without a care in the world. Well, at least I find myself doing that from time to time. You might start to notice a pattern here of pieces with wood bases. With the coffee table, the swivel chair, and the small yellow leopard-print ottoman across from it, I love how the natural wood connects these pieces, making them look as if they are almost floating in the middle of the room.

Speaking of wood, on the wall behind the ottoman is a beautiful walnut credenza (dresser). While the bookshelf on the other side of the room plays a practical role, the credenza brings a sense of sophistication and offers display space. The drawers

CURATED COLLECTION

A ceramic plate sits on our coffee table (opposite). Our bookshelves store a collection of books that we've read and some we've promised ourselves we'll read, a few pieces of art, and random decor elements (right). Above our credenza, this abstract painting of a cat, from friend and artist Jose Mertz, acts as a conversation starter for the room (below).

hold placemats, incense sticks, and—of course—more toys, and I use the open shelves to style books and ceramics. On top of the credenza, I placed a mirror-based lamp, a selection of favorite whiskeys, and, in the center, my chosen book of the week. Above hangs a painting of a cat by artist and friend Jose Mertz—the bold, dynamic energy of the painting balances out the sleek lines of the credenza. On the wall perpendicular to this, I hung a black oak-framed mirror with a fun ripple effect around the edge—just a little something to catch the eye.

While we're on the topic of art, I'd be remiss if I didn't mention the large painting on the wall to the left of the couch. The reason being, well, it's one of my own paintings. All my passions stem from my fine art background, so if I have the space to hang one of my own paintings, I'll take the opportunity. I wanted this piece here because it's bold and bright and has the power to pull you in, and it makes the perfect statement in this room.

When it comes to lighting, the living room should have a warm, enveloping glow. Even though we added recess ceiling lights, I mostly use lamps to create the right mood. Mounted on the wall at one end of the credenza is a vintage black metal wall light that brings a little flair. On top of the rattan-fronted armoire, I've placed a large cylindrical lamp that can be dimmed to produce a gentle glow. Its rope shade complements the rattan of the armoire and introduces yet another natural texture. The dated sconces flanking the large window were replaced with elegant smoked glass ones.

FINE FABRICS

I find bringing in wild prints adds a touch more depth and excitement to a room. This tiger print on an ocher background fabric helps the ottoman from Lulu and Georgia pop (above left). Playing off the tiger print, the digitally styled tiger-striped pillow covers add a bold look when set against the flat gray of the brushed linen fabric of the sofa (left). They even hold their weight next to the red of my painting behind. This textured weave fabric just creates comfort (opposite).

Perfect plants

The living room is typically somewhere many of our statement plants reside and where we do a lot of "living." I threw quotes around that word because, if you're like me, you're mainly assuming a horizontal position when in the living room. As this room is used for relaxing, I love styling plants in here—there is no better way to bring about a sense of calm. However, as I've said before, you have to let the light guide you on the types of plants you can bring into a space. With our living room being mainly north-facing, there is a limited amount of natural light and as a result, I've chosen plants that can tolerate lower amounts of light exposure—snake plants (*Dracaena*), ZZ plants (*Zamioculcas zamiifolia*), a heart-leaf philodendron (*Philodendron hederaceum*) and *P. h.* 'Brasil', an Australian tree fern (*Dicksonia antarctica*), and a lady palm tree (*Rhapis excelsa*).

MY TOP 5 PLANTS TO STYLE IN THE LIVING ROOM

Any ficus tree They create the perfect vibe. Give me a fiddle-leaf fig, an 'Audrey', a benjamina...I'll take them all!

ZZ plant (*Zamioculcas zamiifolia*) This lower-light tolerant beauty fits in any room, but when you sit one in a corner, it instantly lifts that space to the next level.

Ponytail palm (*Beaucarnea recurvata*) You'll need plenty of light for this plant, but it's a good one!

The *Monstera deliciosa* or any of its variegated friends This plant, commonly known as the Swiss cheese plant, is just a tropical vibe setter. The large foliage transports you back to that vacation you spent worry-free, with your hair down and your feet up. Opt for an 'Albo-variegata' or 'Thai Constellation', and you'll have an instant statement piece.

A variegated schefflera, or umbrella plant I mean, duh! Nothing more to be said here.

DESIGNING LIGHTING
HOW THE RIGHT LIGHTING CAN CHANGE THE MOOD OF A ROOM

If you've ever seen the movie *Anchorman*, you'll recognize these three words: "I love lamp!" While it's a hilarious line in the movie, it's also a sentiment most interior lovers would agree with. I do love lamps or, more specifically, designing with light.

The right lighting can set the entire mood and tone of a room, yet for some reason it is one item that is often overlooked or treated as an afterthought when designing a home. Whether it's choosing the placement of recessed lighting or deciding between a floor lamp and a table lamp for a dark corner, keep in mind that thoughtful lighting choices can elevate the design of your home and guide your choices in selecting other decorative elements. Lighting plays a vital role not only in supporting everyday activities but also in enhancing the aesthetic appeal of a room, and getting the lighting right throughout your home will allow you to create the mood you desire. Here are a few tips on what to consider when designing with light.

LIGHT TEMPERATURE

» Have you ever walked into a space and felt the lighting was draining your energy like a mosquito sucking your blood on a summer's day? That can happen if you don't get the color temperature of the lighting right. Light temperature is measured in Kelvins (K). The lower the Kelvin value, the warmer and more yellow the glow of the bulb; the higher the value, the cooler and bluer the light. Understanding which color temperature to choose for each light fixture in a room is essential. Bulbs with a color temperature between 1,000K and 3,200K create a warm, cozy, and calming feeling, while those ranging from 4,000K to 5,000K emit a cooler, whiter light that's crisp and alert. Anything above 5,000K is considered daylight.

» Rooms like the living room, bedroom, kitchen, and dining room—in other words, places where you plan to relax or entertain—should have light fixtures that cast a warmer glow, while cooler lighting

is ideal for task-oriented spaces such as kitchens, bathrooms, laundry rooms, and garages. When choosing light fixtures for a room, think about the function and usage of that space and make sure to choose appropriate bulbs. The one thing I'd warn against is mixing bulbs of different color temperatures in the same room. Wrong is wrong.

RECESSED LIGHTING

» Recessed lighting can be a big design hit or miss, based on how it is used. In the right rooms and for the right purposes it can look great, but when used indiscrimately it can make a room feel overly lit, flat, and draining. Although we have recessed lighting in many of our rooms, I make sure each room also has a good number of floor and table lamps, as we prefer their warmth when settling down to relax with family or guests. But recessed lighting does have its uses. It's especially helpful when a room needs to be brightly illuminated, perhaps during cleaning, or when you want to highlight specific areas—such as artwork on the walls or objects on a shelf.

» Where some people go wrong when renovating is assuming that recessed lighting is necessary to make a room feel complete. While I do believe it can add a clean, modern touch, it can also make a space feel awkward and unbalanced, throwing strange shadows throughout a room. As with

any design choice, it's all about using it intentionally and thoughtfully. One thing I consider absolutely essential when fitting recessed lighting is making sure it is dimmable. This adds flexibility and allows you to adjust the mood in a room as required.

DIMMABILITY

» If you left it up to me, every light fixture would be dimmable, giving you the power to change the mood in a room at the mere flick of a switch. This is especially true in spaces where you're trying to curate a warm and intimate vibe. So, in our living room, bedrooms, and even in the sunroom, I've either purchased fixtures that are dimmable or have connected switches that will allow light levels to be adjusted.

» While dimming the lighting turns down the brightness of the lamps, it can turn up the glow in some of the surrounding fabrics and materials of which your decor pieces are made. I've sat in my sunroom and watched as my *Monstera deliciosa* 'Thai Constellation' went from "cool," while the lamp next to it was at full glow, to "Damn you're fine" once the lamp was dimmed.

STYLED LIGHT

» You can rarely go wrong by having more lamps than you need in a room. I'd rather have the option of turning a few lamps off if a room is too bright than sit in a poorly lit space. I like to style lamps in much the same way I do plants—by layering them and playing around with sizes, shapes, and colors. This layered approach enhances the overall ambience and allows the lighting to adapt to different moods.

» When it comes to layering lamps, it helps to think of it in terms of how you want the light to flow around the room. For example, I will typically have a small portable lamp glowing on a shelf, a table lamp sitting on a side table, a sconce on the wall,

and a floor lamp to one side of the couch. Each lamp is strategically place to create pockets of light at varying heights.

» Varied lamp shapes add character and energy to your space. When choosing fixtures, a lamp's shape and size should complement its placement and surroundings. For example, a globe-shaped lamp pairs better with a curved couch than a standard drum shade, while styling a linear floor lamp next to a bulky couch creates contrast and balance.

The kitchen

Have you ever lived in a house where you wished the kitchen was located where the dining room was? Well, that's exactly how we felt the first time we saw our house. One thing Fiona and I noticed while living in our apartment was that, during parties, everyone always ended up in the kitchen. No matter how small the space, it seemed to be where everyone naturally gathered. Our dining room, on the other hand, was only used occasionally for formal dinners. So when we first viewed this house, we came primed with the knowledge that the kitchen in our "forever home" had to be a place that would allow for everyone to come together comfortably and enjoy spending time.

Concept and moodboard

When we first came to view the house, the kitchen was a small, narrow galley tucked into the northwest corner. Its windows were shaded by a large pine tree just outside, which blocked much of the natural light and made the space feel dark and cramped—definitely not the kitchen of our dreams. In contrast, the dining room was much larger, filled with natural light from its south-facing exposure, and overlooked a private park shared with a small group of neighbors. Fiona and I looked at each other and we both knew exactly what the other was thinking. Yup, we were going to move the kitchen to where the dining room was. I could picture myself sitting by the window with a coffee, gazing out at the park, or calling the kids in for dinner through the open windows. But I'm getting ahead of myself. The kitchen is often called the heart of the home, and we had a lot of work ahead of us to ensure ours lived up to that name.

When designing our new kitchen, the first thing I needed to get a handle on was its tone and feel. This was of the utmost importance as the kitchen would set the design direction for the rest of the house. To lock in the color and material palette, I reflected on the places that brought Fiona and me the most joy. If I could sample the colors from those memories—our wedding in Tulum, Mexico, travels across Europe, and my love of Japanese interiors— they would reflect a calming yet rich aesthetic. We landed on light grays, tans, white, black, and green. For texture, warm woods like red oak and walnut, mixed with concrete, brass, and painted metal. The result would be clean, modern, and inviting.

THE BLANK CANVAS
The dining room as it was when we first bought the house, before it became our kitchen (above left). A pair of French doors divided the then-dining room from the sunroom (above right).

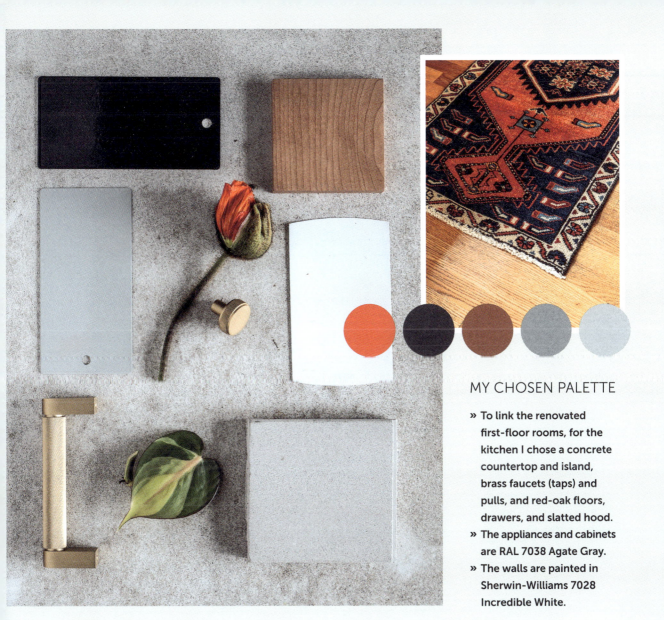

MY CHOSEN PALETTE

» To link the renovated
first-floor rooms, for the
kitchen I chose a concrete
countertop and island,
brass faucets (taps) and
pulls, and red-oak floors,
drawers, and slatted hood.

» The appliances and cabinets
are RAL 7038 Agate Gray.

» The walls are painted in
Sherwin-Williams 7028
Incredible White.

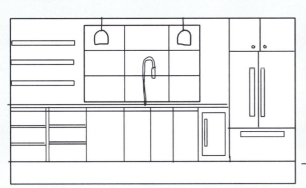

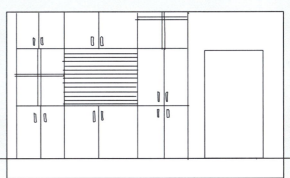

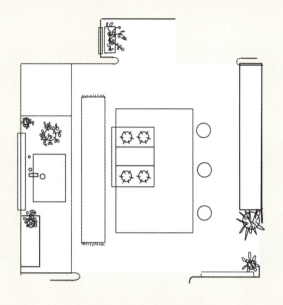

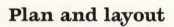

SIZE 217.5 SQ.FT/20.20 SQ.M
CEILING HEIGHT 9 FT/2.7 M
ASPECT SOUTH-FACING

Plan and layout

As we were completely relocating the kitchen, we needed to reroute the existing gas and water lines as well as the ventilation for the cooker hood. We also had to make some other big changes. If you remember, the reason we wanted to move the kitchen was to gain space and take advantage of the south-facing orientation. To make the most of that natural light, we removed the original window and replaced it with one that was more modern, functional, and better suited to the new layout. Because the kitchen countertop would now be installed along the wall where the window sat, our contractors also needed to adjust the height of the new window. Raising it slightly allowed the countertop to fit cleanly and sit just below the windowsill,

While there are standard measurements—like countertop height or refrigerator depth—that you'll need to follow when renovating a kitchen, what truly makes a difference is physically placing yourself in the space before anything is installed. Deciding whether the dishwasher should be on the right or the left of the sink, or if the refrigerator should be on the same side of the room as the range/stove or opposite, can make all the difference to the usability and flow of a kitchen. We've all spent time in a kitchen that just felt "off," right?

Accordingly, after the demolition had taken place, Fiona and I marked the outlines of every cabinet and appliance on the floor with tape. This helped us visualize the layout and make sure everything would feel right in the space. Then we moved around the room, acting out how we'd use the kitchen daily to get a feel for the flow. This step really saved us. It helped us work out how big the island should be, the best spot for the range and refrigerator, and so on. As the

saying goes, "measure twice, cut once." Even if you think you have a good idea of where everything should go, nothing compares to being in the space to get a clear understanding of flow and functionality. Once we'd done this, we knew exactly where we wanted to position everything, so I did a detailed sketch of the layout and sent it to the contractor.

I designed our kitchen to have warm surfaces and soft edges (above). To create a seamless feeling of flow between the dining room, kitchen, and sunroom, I rounded the walls' corners and extended the red-oak wooden slat design throughout.

Cabinets and appliances

We chose all-new red-oak flooring for most of the rooms on the first floor, so I chose to go with red oak for the custom cabinets too. While traveling, I fell in love with the look of Scandinavian and Mexican design and wanted to bring that inspiration into our new home. To achieve this Scandi-Mexican (Sexican, if you will) vibe, I envisaged wood cabinets with clean, simple lines and streamlined integral handles. However, our budget wouldn't allow for fully custom cabinets and we needed to make some compromises. I suggested to our general contractor that he make custom red-oak fronts and pair those with IKEA boxes and drawers behind. I sketched out my ideas and the contractor put together a plan that made it all come to life. They sent over their final layout and went to work.

These drawers are where we keep our dinnerware, flatware, and cloth napkins, and let's not forget the one drawer we all love, the "junk drawer." We were also able to conceal the dishwasher and trash closet behind them. Despite all our careful planning, there ended up being a small gap at the end of the run. When the contractor asked if we wanted to fit in more drawers there, Fiona added her design touch by quickly yelling out "wine fridge." Reason number 421 of why I love her.

On top of the cabinets, we decided on a concrete countertop. I have often admired the look of concrete set against wood, and after seeing the work that Mark Melonas of Luke Works did at Good Neighbor, a local coffee shop here in Baltimore, I asked him to create a custom countertop and

FRUITS OF LABOR
A a vibrant bowl of mandarin oranges makes a kitchen look and smell fresh (right and above right). A gorgeous bouquet of colorful poppies by Pomona Floral are displayed on our kitchen island (opposite).

island for us. Getting to watch Mark craft these pieces was one of my favorite parts of the project. Once the concrete came into the kitchen it was just so beautiful! I love the idea that it will age and develop a patina over time.

For the sink we went with a large white undermount sink and dressed it up with brass features. Above the sink, in front of the window, hang two concrete pendants, chosen to echo the concrete features elsewhere in the kitchen and because the black handle and wire perfectly matched the window frame. When it came to wall storage, we decided floating shelves would be a nice addition. Instead of going with new wood, we asked the team to repurpose some of the headers

removed in the demo. These were planed, sanded, and stained, then secured to the wall using iron rods that were drilled into studs. The team drilled holes into the shelves, which allow the rods to slide into them perfectly, then glued them in place. The shelves are now home to some of our favorite cookbooks, dinnerware, art, and, of course, plants. (See pages 66–67 for guidance on how to style floating shelves.)

The center of the room was the right spot for the island. This is where we imagined gathering with family, where our girls would hang out as we cooked, and where we'd do most of our entertaining. Mark of Luke Works used the same mix and color of concrete to create a countertop for the island—my brief was clean and simple with a waterfall edge.

WILD ON BOTH SIDES

A view of the busiest area of our home (above). We spent time making sure we had placed our appliances correctly in order to create optimal flow. Pops of warm color accent the rich tones of the wooden cabinets and floors. A small Meyer lemon tree, styled in a Mexican pottery planter, brings life to one end of the countertop (opposite).

DESIGN TIP

Getting the layout of a new kitchen right
is important. The key to a feeling of flow
and efficiency is the "work triangle,"
which connects the three most-utilized
areas: the sink, the refrigerator, and the
stove. Plan this right and the way you
move in the kitchen will feel easy and
natural, almost like a dance.

One side of the island is for sitting and the other holds more cabinets and drawers. As we'd moved the range to the island, we had to place an extractor hood above it. But what kind? While I didn't want to go with a standard stainless-steel hood, I did briefly consider a clean white structure protruding from the ceiling. But to unify this room with its neighbors, I decided to incorporate wooden slats in the kitchen too, echoing those present in the powder room and sunroom. This creates a cohesive visual motif that flows seamlessly from the powder room to the kitchen and then into the sunroom. The contractors had to move the vent line from the original kitchen to this position, fitting it between the headers and going out of the western wall. They built the box to hold the vent and cut, sanded, and stained the red-oak slats using the stain Ipswich Pine to match the floors. I love this feature so much. It turned out better than I could have ever imagined and truly feels like a piece of art.

While we're discussing the extractor hood, let's talk about the other appliances too. For these, we went with Bluestar, not only because we loved the look of their range and built-in refrigerators but also because we could select custom colors and trims. We chose RAL 7038 Agate Gray as the color with an antique brass trim. The color of the appliances helped guide our choice for the color of the cabinets too.

One thing Fiona requested in the kitchen was plenty of storage to hide all the usual kitchen clutter so we used the north wall to fulfill this need. We chose a mix of custom red-oak-lined wall cubbies and custom fronts on IKEA boxes.

I designed the wall to our specification and matched the door color to the appliances to ensure a cohesive look. To get a flawless finish on the doors, the contractor had them sprayed at an auto body shop for a perfectly smooth, immaculate look. Honestly, it had me singing Cameo's "Just Like Caaaandy"!

I chose hardware that coordinated with the pulls on the refrigerator and range. Antique brass is a recurring theme throughout the first floor—from the powder room to the sunroom—and it continues throughout the entire house. But the *pièce de resistance* in this room is my appliance garage. I wanted somewhere I could start my daily routine on the perfect note. And to know me is to know I love a good cup of black coffee. We had one of the custom red-oak boxes built with a garage-style door which was painted the same color as the appliances. For the base, we had Mark pour a concrete slab. Now I have my very own coffee station, and one that can be hidden away when necessary.

CUBBIES AND COFFEE

Frequently used cookbooks, a Danish portable cordless table lamp, and a *Stromanthe sanguinea* 'Triostar' in a self-watering glazed ceramic planter are housed in red-oak-lined cubbies. Next to this is what is probably my favorite feature in the whole kitchen—the appliance garage. This holds our espresso machine, grinder, cups, and bags of local Baltimore brand Ceremony Coffee in my favorite flavor Mass Appeal.

Perfect planting

I'd be remiss not to mention the in-floor planter in the kitchen—one of my favorite design features in our entire renovation and a perfect example of how to blur the line between indoors and out.

When we moved the powder room wall, it left a window in the area where the room had previously been. I thought it would be nice to replace this with a larger window to let light flow into the new kitchen. And when we realized we needed new wood flooring on the first floor, it gave me the perfect opportunity to add an in-floor planter, which I decided to place in front of this window.

I initially planted a calamansi tree (*Citrus* x *microcarpa* here, but when our older daughter, Holland, became mobile, she began to pull off the fruit. These were very small and I was nervous that she would swallow them, so it was time to remove the plant until she got a little older. Thankfully, we had thought ahead and had a cover made from leftover flooring to fit the planter hole, so it can be covered when necessary. Now Holland is older, she no longer tries to eat soil or stones and the planter is back in use. To avoid having the same issue when Vada starts crawling, I decided to plant a taller, more established Meyer lemon tree, so the fruits are out of her reach. If you're wondering, we keep a small dustpan and brush nearby to clean up any dirt that finds its way outside the planter, which drains out directly into our plumbing line.

LEMON PEPPER

Our cat Pepper takes in the view from the window (above left). I designed a cover for the in-floor planter in our kitchen, so we can cover it over when it's not in use (left). The planter in action (opposite). Soaking up the warm southern light, our large Meyer lemon tree is starting to develop new buds.

When it comes to styling plants in the kitchen, I'm of the opinion that if you have the light and the space, then fill it with plants. If the light is right, the kitchen is one of the best rooms in the home to style plants because, well, there's easy access to water right there at the sink. While I already have one Meyer lemon in the in-floor planter, I couldn't resist having another on the countertop. I styled this in a clay face planter, giving it instant personality. Behind that, growing up a stake, is a *Philodendron brandtianum*. To bring life to narrow corners in your home, try using moss poles or stakes to support climbing vines. On the other side of the sink, on the floating shelves, I've styled a *Hoya carnosa* and a *Philodendron hederaceum* 'Brasil'. Their vines tumble down the shelves and some have even clambered onto the pendant light. On the other side of the room, I've placed a *Dracaena trifasciata* subsp. *trifasciata* in one of my black geometric planters and in one of the wall cubbies a *Stromanthe sanguinea* 'Triostar'.

The heart of our home was complete, and it was everything we wanted. What I learned when renovating a home is that you'll be forced to make budget compromises, but you must consider the safety of those who live in the home first. Renovating can be stressful, but when you see the vision start to come alive it's an incredible feeling.

WILD AT HOME
Moving our kitchen to this side of the house was one of the best decisions we made when renovating. The southern light makes it warm, welcoming, and lush with plants (above). A painting from Alina Fassakhova shines out bold and bright.

TOP 5 MUST-HAVES
WHEN PLANNING A KITCHEN

Appliance garage There are must-haves and then there are MUST-HAVES and an appliance garage is the latter. In our kitchen, I made sure to include one to use as a little coffee nook. It keeps the countertop tidy and gives you the option to tuck away appliances when needed.

Citrus tree Imagine if you walked into your kitchen to be greeted by the sweet floral scent of a blooming citrus tree. Yes, that could be yours with just a little direct sun and regular watering.

Extra storage Which room couldn't use a little extra storage? You might think your space is enough for just you and your spouse, but as your family grows, you'll need more storage.

Dimmable lighting Your next dinner party is probably going to end up in the kitchen, and if your lights are too bright, that cool party vibe just isn't going to happen. Fitting dimmable lighting will allow you to change the mood and feel of your kitchen at the flick of a switch.

Deep sink It may not be the mind-blowing suggestion you were expecting, but I've been in enough kitchens to know that a deep sink is a feature that's often overlooked. Beyond just washing dishes, our deep sink has been used for everything, from watering plants to thawing out a large Thanksgiving turkey. One of my favorite memories is giving our firstborn, Holland, a bath in that very sink when she was an infant.

STYLING FLOATING SHELVES

When it comes to kitchen design, floating shelves are one of the most sought-after features. While wall cabinets will play a role in many kitchens, they can feel bulky and weighty. Replacing them with floating shelves opens up the space, creating a lighter, brighter atmosphere. They also have a practical role to play, making it easy to access tableware you use every day while showing off a curated collection of favorite items. It's this blending of functionality and style that makes them so versatile.

The one drawback of opting for floating shelves over wall cabinets is that anything placed on them remains visible and on display. As a result, an untidy or cluttered shelf can easily detract from the overall appearance of the kitchen. Here are a few tips on how to style floating shelves with confidence.

» Empty the shelves, then measure the height, width, and length to get a sense of the space you are working with. This will help you choose the pieces to include.

» Once I'm familiar with the dimensions of the shelves, I gather together the pieces I intend to display. Of course, the shelves will hold glasses and dishware, but what makes them unique and special is the addition of those fun pieces that tell a story about the individuals who live in the home.

» When the shelves are empty, think of them as a blank canvas. As you begin to style them, it's important to consider the overall composition. In this case, we're focusing on creating balance. Start by placing the foundational pieces—items that will visually ground the shelves. These are objects like vases, framed art, sculptures, and books. I place one of these anchor pieces on each shelf, preferably at different ends to create a nice sense of balance.

» As I add items, I consider color, texture, and the story they tell—this helps guide me in creating a strong and visually compelling arrangement. The last thing you want your floating shelves to be is boring or cluttered. Make sure you're picking pieces that fit your overall aesthetic, and don't be afraid to edit as you go. Remember, everything on the shelves will always be on show.

» One way to make sure that your shelves are eye-catching for all the right reasons is to include items of varying heights,

make sure the arrangement reflects the style and feeling I want to convey. The thing that many people have a hard time doing when styling floating shelves, or styling in general, is editing. Coco Chanel once said that before leaving the house she always removed one item, and that's a great approach to take when you're styling a shelf. It's OK not to have every single inch filled. So, if the shelf doesn't feel balanced or needs a little room to breathe, just remove something.

shapes, and materials. This means if I'm placing a tall, slender piece, I'll balance it with a shorter round object.

» Once I've added the larger pieces, and worked out where the everyday tableware will go, I'll introduce a plant or two. As with any area in your home, plants need light to thrive, so be sure to choose varieties that suit the specific lighting conditions of the room. While small or slow-growing plants work well in the center of a shelf, floating shelves with open ends are calling out for trailing plants like hoyas and philodendrons.

» As the final stage, I assess the overall picture and add small details for pops of color and a touch of attitude. Then I'll stand back and take a last look to

The dining room

Is it just me, or is the formal dining room a thing of the past? Don't get me wrong, I love the idea of a traditional dining room where we all gather around the table to eat with family and friends. But those perfectly pristine spaces, dedicated only to formal events or special occasions, are now "gone like the winters of yesteryear." Well, at least in my home they are. For us, the dining room is a room to enjoy every day; somewhere to eat dinner at night, with guests or just the family, where our kids can do homework or work on school projects, and a place to play games or build puzzles. So when we first came to see the house, we knew just what we were looking for in a dining room.

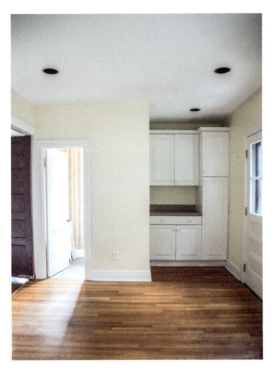

Concept and moodboard

When we decided to move the original dining room to where the kitchen was and vice versa, our intention was not to create a traditional formal dining room. Instead, the goal was to create an interior that was welcoming and stylish rather than stiff or precious in any way. While we hoped that our new dining room would provide a backdrop for many special family moments and enduring memories yet to be made, we were also aware that out of all the rooms in our home, this one will probably be utilized the least. Although we plan to sit around the table here many times a week, for the most part busy family daily living takes place in the other rooms in the house.

To maintain a consistent look and feel throughout our first-floor renovations, we chose to use the same materials and colors in every room. For instance, if we incorporated concrete elements in the kitchen, you'll also notice concrete details carried into the dining room. Since the entire house is painted white, I expected that much of the color and energy in each room would come from the decor. For the dining room, I put together a palette that included shades of gray, green, and black, and pops of brighter colors introduced through artwork. When it came to materials and textures, I envisioned a mix of concrete, various woods, jute, and brass. The new red-oak wood flooring that runs throughout the first floor brings a sense of warmth and depth which grounds the dining room. Together, these elements would help create the atmosphere we wanted for the space.

THE BLANK CANVAS

This is how our current dining room looked as a kitchen before the renovation (above). We decided to move the kitchen to the other side of the house as, being on the north-west side, the room felt too dark and moody for a kitchen but just right for a dining room.

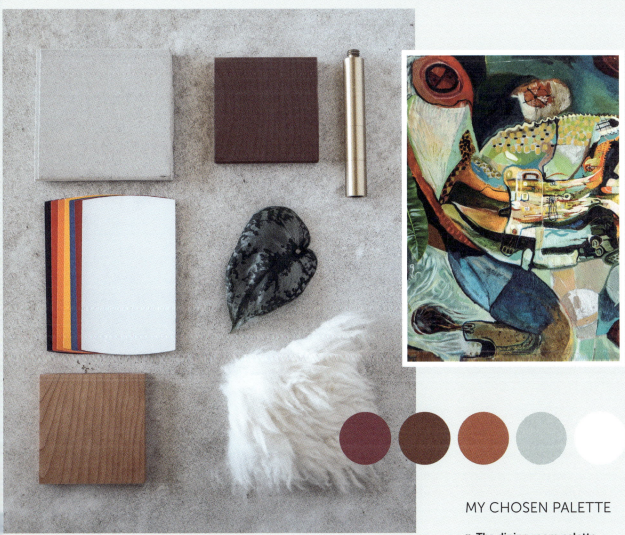

MY CHOSEN PALETTE

» The dining room palette reflects the choices used in the kitchen, sunroom, and powder room.

» With the walls being painted in Sherwin-Williams 7028 Incredible White and the ceiling in 7007 Ceiling Bright White, the bright colors of the room come from the large painting by Jose Mertz.

» Textures of concrete, brass, and walnut echo the rest of the first floor.

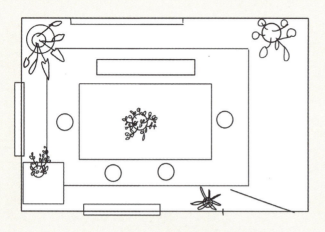

SIZE 165 SQ FT/15.3 SQ.M
CEILING HEIGHT 9 FT/2.7 M
ASPECT NORTH- & WEST-FACING

Plan and layout

As I've mentioned before (see page 52), when we first visited the house, this room was a galley kitchen, with appliances and cabinets lining the walls. Knowing that it would become our new dining room, the next step was clear. Yes, that's right—rip out the entire room. Compared to the other rooms on the first floor—where the renovation involved moving walls, creating entirely new layouts, and installing all-new built-ins—our new dining room was fairly simple. Well, simple enough. The removal of the existing kitchen required the disconnection and rerouting of the the plumbing and gas lines to the new kitchen. Once that was completed, however, everything came together smoothly.

We continued the same red-oak flooring from the kitchen, entryway, and living room into the dining room. As there was no longer a kitchen countertop here, we were able to make the new windows slightly larger, as in the living room and other rooms in the house. Once those jobs were complete, the walls went up and we had our new dining room. Just as I said, simple enough. The beauty of the room would come from the styling.

CENTERPIECE

Here is a glimpse of the finished dining room. Mixing materials is one of the easiest ways to add life to a room. The concrete table acts as a stand for the gorgeous arrangement by Sarah Ruberto of Pomona Floral, a local Baltimore floral artist. On the wall is a painting by my good friend Jose Mertz. With the painting being so energetic, I felt I could keep everything else in the room calm.

Furniture

As this space is all about gathering with others around the table, finding the right one was important. We envisioned a table that would comfortably sit eight people, with a simple design, a modern aesthetic, and materials that echoed those used throughout the rest of the first floor. My first impulse was to purchase a concrete table that I'd seen online. But when I received the concrete sample, it wasn't a good match in color or texture for the custom concrete pieces we had installed in the kitchen and powder room. Fiona suggested asking Mark from Luke Works, who made our concrete island, countertop, and vanity, if he would consider making a table for us too. This way, the color and texture would be aligned with the other concrete pieces in the house.

While making tables wasn't something that Mark did often, he understood what we wanted and thought it was a great idea. Before this, I had rarely considered having local makers build custom pieces for our home, thinking there would be a big difference in cost, lead times, and so on. However, I discovered that working with a local creator doesn't necessarily mean the item will cost more than you'd pay when purchasing from a big brand. What it does mean is that you're supporting the local economy and having something special and unique created for your space. For us, it's the work of talented artists and creators that truly makes this home uniquely ours. To go with our new table, I chose sleek mid-century wooden dining chairs and

DEEP IN DETAILS
A snapshot of the design of the dining room (above). From the floral centerpiece on the table to the snake plant on the floor, there is life popping into view from every corner of this space. The walnut detail of the dining chairs and a detail of the walnut from the hanging fixture (opposite above left and right). These Stokke highchairs are great because they can be converted into regular chairs as our girls grow (opposite below).

a sturdy wooden bench. Beneath the table, a large jute rug adds texture and a natural element to the space, while also helping to conceal the spills and wear and tear that are bound to happen when dining with children.

For lighting, we had recessed lighting fitted in the ceiling and I added a slim, linear LED chandelier made with walnut wood which follows the length of the table. I saw this fixture online and loved the way the linear shape curves slightly in the middle, creating a soft moment in a hard line. On the north wall of the room, to the left side of the window, I styled a wood and white marble bar cabinet. This is where we store extra barware and glassware and, of course, a few special bottles.

Creative greenery

While most of the walls in this room are occupied by windows or doors, there is one blank wall and here I've hung a painting by Jose Mertz (see pages 72–73). I've had this artwork for 25 years and knew it would make a statement here. Just like his work in the living room, this large-scale piece shows Jose's masterful use of rich color to meld together his abstract forms. Next to it is a small pop art-style painting by artist Lolo Gem. These works brought the vibrant pops of color that the room needed to elevate its energy, and I knew that incorporating plants would add the perfect finishing touch.

On the top of the streamlined wood and marble bar cabinet, I styled a satin pothos (*Scindapsus pictus* 'Argyraeus') which cascades out of a concrete planter and tumbles down the side of the cabinet. To the right side of the window is a *Philodendron billietiae* in a brass planter on a black lacquer pedestal. This combination of planter and pedestal also appears in the sunroom and I repeated it here to pull the rooms together. In the opposite corner, the leaves of a variegated *Dracaena trifasciata* subsp. *trifasciata* bring a burst of glossy color.

A LESSON IN LIGHT

The dining room window beams with morning light, allowing the room and everything in it to glow (above). The shadows stretch across the table around the centerpiece, spotlit as the star of the room. Even though some corners of the room are darker than others, the overall daylight brightens the space hugely.

TABLE STYLING

Creating the perfect table setting is all about adding layers (above, left, and opposite). Each little detail, such as a rattan placemat below ceramic plates and gold flatware, creates a festive holiday setting. One thing you can do to make your table stand out during a dinner party is ensure it has a centerpiece. Depending on the occasion, I like to get a floral artist to design something special for the table.

TOP 5 WAYS TO ELEVATE A TABLE SETTING

Centerpiece A gorgeous, sculptural centerpiece is an instant eyecatcher and will leave your guests in awe. The one downside of this beauty is that it will need to find another spot once the dinner begins because you don't want it creating barriers.

Menus This isn't just a nice touch—it's an amazing touch! A touch that will take your dinner party to the next level. Your guests aren't expecting it, so when they see it, they feel special.

Stylish glassware When it comes to glassware, being intentional with your selection for the evening festivities will make the difference. Whether based on the type of beverage you'll be serving that evening or chosen according to your color palette, it brings elegance to the table setting.

Folded napkins This doesn't mean the basic rectangular napkin fold. I'm talking about the ones that take more time to whip up. Fancy folds will bring a little dimension and additional layers to your table.

Candles Make it a classic night and have a candlelit dinner. There is no better way to create ambience and mood than to light a few pillar candles during a dinner party.

The powder room

While many of us have powder rooms in our homes today, we don't use them to "powder" our noses—that's just an old term that has stuck around for centuries. Nowadays, a powder room is more commonly known as a half-bathroom, consisting of a toilet and sink, and is somewhere guests go to "freshen up." It may be a small room—possibly even the smallest room in the house—but it's likely to have a lot of visitors. If you're looking to redesign or renovate a room in your home, the powder room is the perfect candidate. It might be a small space, but it can have a big impact.

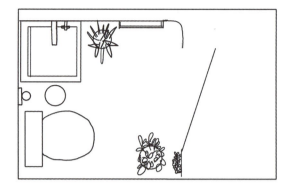

SIZE 18 SQ FT/1.7 SQ M
CEILING HEIGHT 8 FT 5 IN/2.5 M
ASPECT SOUTH-FACING

THE BLANK CANVAS

An image of how the powder room looked when we purchased the house (left). Everything in it felt dated and the goal, as with the entire home, was to create a new space with flow and purpose.

Concept and moodboard

When we first viewed this house, the powder room was located by the original galley kitchen. It was the perfect size, but very much stuck in the wrong era. As was the case with pretty much every other room in the house, the decor was completely out of date. Additionally, as we were planning to move the kitchen to the other side of the house, the powder room was now, by default, situated in the wrong spot. In its original location, there were kitchen cabinets positioned between it and the corner of the house. But now, the decision to relocate the kitchen gave us the opportunity to slide the powder room neatly into a corner of the house, making the flow from the kitchen into the dining room feel seamless and uninterrupted.

Plan and layout

Our plan to reposition the powder room by about 5ft/1.5m would require a few plumbing changes but didn't pose too much of a challenge for the contractors. As the original room had a small window, once it was moved, it left a window between the kitchen and the dining room. Now, as you already know, I'll take as many windows in the house as possible, so this was another one of those "good" problems to have (see pages 62–63 to see how I treated this window). As a result, we needed to add a window in the new powder room. Once we knew where this would go, I sketched out a layout. When a powder room is located in or near your kitchen, making sure it's well laid out is key. Put plainly, no one wants to look at a toilet while sitting at the kitchen table, so when designing the floor

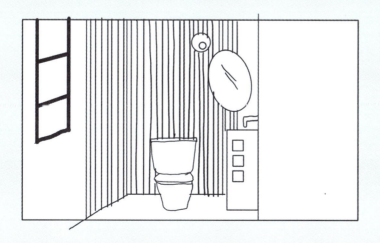

MY CHOSEN PALETTE

» The colors and textures used in the kitchen and sunroom continue here.

» Tile: Fireclay triangle tiles (Calcite, Desert Bloom, Dolomite, Tumbleweed, Magnetite).

» Paint: Sherwin Williams Incredible White.

» Textures: Red oak slats, concrete for the sink and vanity from Lukeworks, CB2 marble sconce, brushed brass for the Phylrich faucet and waste basket, glazed ceramic, terra-cotta, and plant life.

GAME OF TONES

The finished powder room (right). Creating a more modern and refined look for the house meant swapping out a few things, including the toilets. The tone of this space is warm and inviting (opposite). Every decision on color and texture played a role in making a small space feel large.

plan for this room, I placed the toilet in the corner of the room, just about out of view when the powder room door is open.

Again, I chose tile flooring from Fireclay Tile for this room, in order to create a sense of connection between the rooms on the first floor. Using the colors of the sunroom tile as a guide, I switched it up by adding a few darker shades and changing the shape of the tile. Here, I went with a triangle-shaped tile and designed it so that when four of them came together to make a square, three of the four tiles would always be the same color. While this might not be obvious to a guest entering the room, it was something I carefully mapped out for the installer. But even with a map to lead them, the installers still got it wrong in certain areas. As I have mentioned elsewhere, don't hold anything too precious with a reno, because something will almost certainly not go to plan. Save some space for grace.

The next thing to go in was the red-oak slats. Once I made the decision to have them in the sunroom, I knew I wanted them in the powder room too. While the slats cover the ceiling in the sunroom, here I decided to use them as an accent on the wall, tying the two rooms together. I'm a huge fan of symmetry, but I love when something feels slightly off or organic. So, instead of having one wall completely covered in slats, I shifted them over slightly and had some spill around the corner onto the next wall as well, to create an off-centered effect. This left a neat little corner that was just the right size for the vanity unit.

Fixtures and fittings

Continuing with the same materials used in the kitchen and sunroom, again we called on Mark of Lukeworks to build the vanity. I sketched out the look I had in mind and sent it over to him. When choosing the color of the concrete, I requested something on the lighter side to keep the room brighter and asked for a finish that was raw and textural. Unlike the kitchen countertop and island, where the concrete is smooth and clean, I wanted the vanity to have imperfections, like bubbles and a chipped-like edge. This unfinished effect would complement the clean lines of the slats.

When working with such a small room, smart ways to utilize space are key. I decided to design built-in cubbies below the basin to hold hand towels and candles. This small-space planning came into effect again when considering the faucet (tap). I have always loved the look of a wall-mounted

faucet, and going with a single cross handle felt right. The brass finish is repeated in the kitchen faucet and elsewhere in the decor as well.

As the faucet is wall-mounted, a back splash was needed. Instead of taking the concrete up to the faucet, I decided it would look cleaner if it extended to cover the height of the wall, filling the space between the wooden slats and the flanking wall. Now we had a wall full of texture, weight, and pop! But we also had many vertical lines, and I wanted to break that up. I found a mirror on Etsy that was large enough to overlap both slats and concrete, breaking up the hard lines. The organic shape of the mirror reminded me of a droplet of water, so it felt just right. To add a little touch of mood lighting, I placed a round marble sconce with a single opaque white glass globe to the top left of the mirror, fixing it directly onto the slats. The sconce adds a soft, organic look to the room and brings a new texture to the first floor. In terms of the design of this room, it felt like the dot on an "i" or, better yet, the period at the end of a sentence, because it was the perfect last touch. Period.

With the powder room right next to the kitchen, we wanted to make it as unobtrusive as possible, and to achieve this, we went with a seamless door, meaning it doesn't have a frame around it, as traditional doors do. This was just one of the many small details we added to make the house feel new.

CLEAN LINES

It's important to be deliberate with the decisions you're making when designing a home (above left). The same textures and materials are seen here and elsewhere in the house. A view right outside of the powder room (left). Having a frameless door makes the room feel sleek and unobtrusive. With limited space, wall planters are key (opposite left). Cubbies in the vanity can hold a lot (opposite right).

Small space, small plants

As this is a small space, I couldn't add as much plant life as we typically have in other rooms throughout our house. However, I did see an opportunity in the vertical space, planting a *Hoya linearis* and a *Peperomia tetragona* in ceramic wall planters from my first collection with Target. Tucked into a corner, in a terra-cotta planter, stands a *Dracaena*. With its upright form, this doesn't take up too much precious floor space.

TOP 5 MUST-HAVES IN A POWDER ROOM

Scented candles Listen, we all know what goes down in there. Placing a scented candle in the powder room keeps it smelling fresh while adding a gentle flicker of ambience.

Hand lotion If you're looking to "class up" your powder room, make sure it has a bottle of lotion next to the soap. Clean and moisturized hands go hand in hand. Yeah, I said that.

Extra hand towels Whether you place them in a small bin, a basket, or in little cubbies as I have, putting additional hand towels in your powder room gives guests the option to start with one that's fresh and dry and helps the planet by not using paper. It's a win-win.

Plunger Look, I know it's not the most appealing item to have in the powder room but, trust me, your guests would rather see it there than feel embarrassed when they have to ask you for it. Bonus points added if you make sure there are extra rolls of TP.

Small plant A little green life goes a long way. Something low maintenance, like a snake plant or succulent, would suffice.

The sunroom

The goal of a sunroom is to blur the line between the indoors and out, providing a space that is bright, inviting, and, most importantly for me, lush. This is a space where windows are abundant, allowing the perfect view of the outside environment while keeping you cozy indoors. Here we can sit comfortably with a favorite book (maybe one of mine) and watch a dramatic rainstorm or feel the welcome warmth of the sun caressing our skin on a winter's day. If the kitchen is the heart of the home, the sunroom is undoubtedly its soul, a space for contemplation, rejuvenation, and reflection. All these thoughts were foremost in my mind when I came to design this space.

THE BLANK CANVAS

Views of the sunroom before renovation (left). While the room was ready to be lived in, many things weren't right for the new space—the carpeted floor, eggshell walls, and fixed windows made the room feel stale and bland. The plan was for me to fill it with life.

Concept and moodboard

The perfect sunroom should evoke the feelings of calm, comfort, and warmth you feel when you're forest bathing and stretch your arms out, so leaves brush against your fingers. Or the feeling of relaxing on a beach, watching the fronds of a palm dance above, while listening to the sound of waves crashing onto the sand. It sounds poetic because it should be poetic. This room is supposed to be a getaway, a sanctuary, and I wanted to fill it with plants and more plants—thanks to the great light, this had the potential to become the lushest room in our home. And as with any room where a lot of moisture may come into contact with the floor, a tile floor would be the most practical solution.

Different hues of brown, white, green, orange, and black are as prevalent here as textures of wood, terra-cotta, stone, and leafy greenery, and you'll see this represented in my designs for the ceiling, planters, and other decor here. The aim was simply to give this room a heartbeat, make it feel alive. This is what I imagined when I pictured a sunroom and what I dreamed of when I imagined my very own.

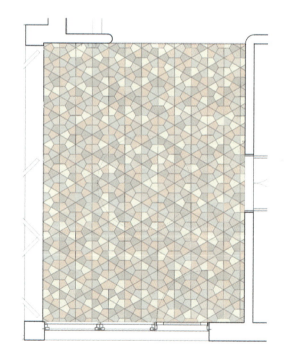

TILING PLAN

I created this layout to give the tiler a map of how I wanted the floor to look, given that each color was laid in a particular orientation. The tile is from Fireclay Tile of California.

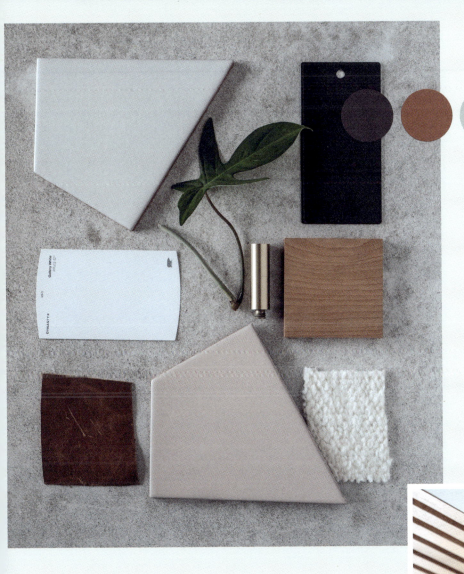

MY CHOSEN PALETTE

» The idea of blurring the
line between indoor and
out was explored here.

» Like the other walls on the
first floor, the walls were
painted in Sherwin-Williams
7028 Incredible White.

» Earthy tones like gray,
ivory, pink, and brown
were used for the tile floor.
The ceiling has red-oak
wooden slats. Other
textures include terrazzo,
leather, terra-cotta, and
greenery growing wild.

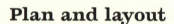

SIZE 171 SQ FT/15.9 SQ M
CEILING HEIGHT 9 FT/2.7 M
ASPECT SOUTH- & EAST-FACING

Plan and layout

If you follow me on social media or have read my book *Living Wild*, you'll be familiar with the sunroom I designed for our home, because I've shared it more than any other space in our home. Do you remember the scene in *The Lion King* when baby Simba is presented to the crowd from the top of Pride Rock? Well, that's how I like to show off our sunroom. For me, it's the *pièce de résistance* of our home.

When Fiona and I first toured the house, I wasn't aware that it even had a sunroom because it didn't appear in the listing. However, when we walked through the front door, I found myself instinctively gliding toward this space as if it was pulling me in. The first thing I identified was that it was east- and south-facing. Having any sunroom is wonderful, but a south-facing one is special, as it receives abundant sunlight. I thought about all the plants I could style here and how they'd thrive. Honestly, it was enough

to make me want to sign the deed that very day. The only drawback was the way the room looked. The windows were wrong, the floor was carpeted, and the built-in bookshelves and ceiling fan were dated. But I was so in love with the idea of this room that I could see past these flaws and focus entirely on its potential instead. I knew exactly what to do here—I just needed to pull it all together.

Like the kitchen, dining room, and powder room, we gutted the sunroom completely. And just as we chose to open up the space between the kitchen and dining room by removing the wall dividing them, I decided to remove the wall and French doors that separated the sunroom and the kitchen in order to create a seamless flow between the three spaces. However, we kept the original French doors separating the sunroom from the living room. The built-in bookshelves and a radiator concealed in one of the bookshelves were removed to give us more space. To replace this heat source, we installed a mini-split air conditioning and heater unit in the ceiling. And, of course, the sun's warmth flows into this room all day long.

The contractors started by removing the existing floor and installing a new one that was level with the rest of the first floor. You see, at some point in its life the original sunroom was a screened-in porch built on a concrete base with side drainage to let water escape. Though it was later enclosed to become part of the house and the drainage sealed, the original flooring remained unchanged.

Once the floor was level, the contractors were ready to start tiling. I had a vision of something fresh and cool with a mixture of interestingly shaped tiles

in various colors, and to fit this brief I chose the Hexite tile from Fireclay Tile of California. I fell in love with its geometric shape and chose six colors: Feldspar, Tumbleweed, Ivory, Dolomite, Chateau, and Halite—basically a combination of white, gray, tan, and muted terra-cotta. To cover the entire floor was going to require a lot of tile and time, so I drew up a plan of where I wanted each tile to go and gave it to the installer to use as a guide

LUSH AND LIGHT
The sunroom after renovation, prior to styling (opposite). The vibrant room in all its peaceful, morning glory (below). The floor-to-ceiling windows bring in gentle light, nourishing all the plants in this space and linking the room to the outside greenery.

(see page 90). While it may have looked a little random, there was a method to my randomness: all six colors would come together to make up the hexagon at the center of the room. After all my planning, this concept mattered to me—so when the installer used the wrong tile colors, despite the map I provided, I was frustrated. Still, I learned an important lesson: don't get too precious during a renovation. You need to roll with the mistakes and find a way to make them work.

The next step was to replace the windows and doors. The old windows were fixed shut and covered with a filter gel that gave warm daylight a cool blue tint. Not ideal for a space where I wanted to house plenty of plants that require sun and air flow. And the small door leading to the backyard was broken. My plan was to have glass windows and doors from ceiling to floor on both the exterior walls. On the east-facing wall, we replaced the small existing door with a large glass door and two large windows. We took out the entire south-facing wall and replaced it with accordion-style glass doors and an additional swinging glass door. Now the room would be flooded with light from top to bottom. We chose accordion doors with the vision of building a deck just outside, allowing the doors to fold back completely and open the room to the outdoors. I could see myself pulling them open and stepping straight onto the deck, seamlessly blending indoor and outdoor living.

While each room in our home has its own individual design story, I think it's important to find creative ways to tie them together, whether by having a consistent color palette, a design statement or a recurring motif. When it came to our home, I considered how to connect the living spaces and

decided on red-oak slats as the design statement. Since we were using them on one wall of the powder room, I thought applying them to the sunroom ceiling would create a wow factor. There has been an uptick in how designers treat ceilings over the past decade, and I have jumped aboard that bandwagon. The slatted ceiling immediately draws the eye upward, allowing everyone that enters the room to take in the entire space.

In the center of the ceiling, I placed a new black fan, chosen to match the trim of the windows and doors and stand out against the warm wood. Similarly, a white mini-split unit is recessed into the ceiling. The fan circulates air—essential for a room full of plants—while the mini-split controls the temperature. Removing the original radiator gained some space but lost heat, so fitting the mini-split between the ceiling joists maintains a clean look without sacrificing heating or cooling.

To finish the ceiling off, recessed lighting was added. Positioned between the slats in the same path as the recessed lighting in the kitchen, this provides a warm, welcoming glow that draws you into the room.

PEPPER AND POPPIES
Removing the French doors from the kitchen into the sunroom allows the glow of the sunroom to creep into the kitchen (opposite). Our cat Pepper sits in Holland's chair, taking in the warmth (above). The brass threshold between both rooms creates a more elegant transition between the wood floors and the tile and echoes the brass touches found in each room (right).

SECRET LIFE OF LEAVES

The largest *Monstera deliciosa* 'Thai Constellation' from my collection (above). You can tell the maturity of the leaves from the number of fenestrations they have. The same plant, with a few of the leaves showing brown spots—a sign of natural decay (above left). There is beauty in nature's design, which is why I chose to leave this leaf alone. A variegated *Ficus binnendijkii* 'Alii' styed in a rippled brass planter (left).

A wild interior

The new sunroom was everything we had hoped for. Honestly, it was better than I had imagined—bright, inviting, and refreshing. The only things it needed were furniture and plants. But not in that order. Unlike other rooms in the house, where I start by styling the furniture and then bringing in plants as accent pieces, in the sunroom, the plants are the main event. And knowing that this room would be full of bright indirect light with a mix of direct sunlight, the world was my oyster when it came to selecting plants to style here.

With the goal of making the sunroom the lushest room in the house, I wanted every surface to provide a home for greenery. You see, when I go about styling an interior with plants, I choose the plants based on the feelings and memories that they evoke. I don't just select them randomly. For instance, one plant that I include in almost all my own spaces is the *Monstera deliciosa*. Its large, split-leaf foliage never fails to pull me back to the day I married my wife in a jungle in Tulum, Mexico. Whatever type of day I'm having, even if it's stressful or sad, when I sit near a monstera, I am transported back to my wedding day and that feeling is washed away. Be intentional when selecting your plants and understand how they can affect the emotions of the individuals who will be nurtured by them.

In the main corner of the room, in front of the two fixed windows, I styled a large *Monstera deliciosa* 'Thai Constellation' in a warm white planter from my third Target collection, stacked on top of another of the same planters. To give it even more height, I placed it on a concrete and wood plant stand, making this the statement plant in the room. Below the monstera, I styled a variegated *Philodendron giganteum* 'Marble', a large *Philodendron mayoi*, a *Philodendron* 69686 and a *Monstera deliciosa* 'Albo-Variegata', which some might argue is the true statement plant in the room. This grouping quickly set the tone of the room.

Directly across from this grouping, I placed a variegated *Ficus binnendijkii* 'Alii' in a rippled brass planter and styled it on top of a black lacquer plant stand. I tucked it into the corner to bring a touch of green but also to pull the view to the gleam of brass, ensuring that the full room is seen. Below it I styled a large ZZ plant (*Zamioculcas zamiifolia*) in a black-coated terra-cotta pot and above this pair, covering the wall, I hung a few mounted plants. Playing with vertical space when styling plants is a technique I love because it mimics the way we interact with plants outdoors. The plants on the wall here are mounted directly on wood planks or in cork, which pushes them out into the room as if they are growing from trees. Now I had found the right home for the core plants in the room, it was time to make some decisions on where the furniture should go.

LUSH LIVING

One way to make a room feel lush is to use the vertical space for plant styling (opposite). Here, I've created a "living wall" of mounted plants. Many of them are mounted on wood boards with cork attached to them, giving a depth to the room that a standard potted plant can't. Dancing lady orchid, polka dot begonia (*Begonia maculata*), *Philodendron mayoi,* and a *Labisia* 'Kura Kura' (above, clockwise from top right).

STYLE TIP

My go-to method for plant styling is to create
layers of greenery of different shapes, sizes, and
colors, replicating the way plants grow in the wild
and instantly making your indoor space feel lush.
The way a monstera creates a canopy over a
philodendron transports you to a tropical jungle.
But the overall impact also depends on the
planters you choose to style plants in.

DECOR AND MORE

I started the styling of the sunroom with the plants first, but every other piece of decor had to add to the idea of bringing the outside in—here a brass cactus-shaped lamp sits among the real plants (left). A living wall created with propagations (opposite above). This walnut bookshelf still feels like it's in its natural habitat (opposite below).

Furniture

Given that the sunroom is directly next to the living room, I wanted to give them two distinct personalities in terms of design. As the living room is somewhere everyone can come together and relax, I felt the sunroom should be therapeutic and zen-like. Instead of a couch, this room has accent chairs that invite you to read a book, have a cup of tea, or enjoy a nightcap. I went with two modern leather chairs as the centerpiece of the room, adding a sense of sophistication. These chairs have traveled with me from previous homes, and when we started the renovation, I knew they would find their place in the sunroom. One of my favorite features is how the fluted detail of the chair backs mimics the slats in the ceiling.

Beside each chair is an acacia-wood side table with a sculptural twisted design. One table is home to a modern brass table lamp with several arms which are reminiscent of a cactus. In the center

of the room, I positioned an ivory shag rug with a modern abstract black-lined design and on top is a round black terrazzo coffee table. Terrazzo is a beautiful stone and brings subtle yet intriguing pattern to a room. This is a timeless piece, so we'll always have a place for it, regardless of how we update this space. I've used the color black to encourage the eye to travel around the room, from the window frames to the coffee table to the ceiling fan, creating a pleasing balance.

On the coffee table, I've created a centerpiece with a potted polka dot begonia (*Begonia maculata*) alongside books and candles. On the other side of the coffee table, facing the accent chairs, I provided a small kid's lounger for our toddler to nestle into, so we can gather in the room as a family. Details like this tell your children that the space they live in is also somewhere they can thrive. Across from the coffee table, along the wall, I've added a sleek walnut

bookshelf to hold a few favorite art and design books, a vintage sculpture, and a few bottles of alcohol, in case the mood strikes. Last, but not least, on the wall closest to the kitchen, I created a living wall using cuttings from plants that I've propagated. I call these walnut vessels "cradles," and each holds four glass test tubes housing plant cuttings. When styling a wall like this, I like to use different types of plants, so the wall has a lush and wild look.

What I absolutely love about the sunroom is that it's the one room in our home that is forever changing. Whether it's thanks to the plants, the view of the trees outside as the seasons change, or the occasional swap of a chair or piece of decor, this room just feels alive.

TOP 5 MUST-HAVES IN A SUNROOM

Plants, plants, and, did I forget to mention, more plants! You could have guessed that this would be at the top of the list. While a sunroom suggests it might have sun, the one MUST is plants. If not, you're living wrong.

Ceiling fan Not only does this keep the room cool, it also circulates the air, helping your plants to breathe and keeping pests like gnats and mosquitoes away.

The perfect shades While letting light in is key, being able to control those light levels is everything.

Tile floor Visually, tile helps to break up wood or concrete flooring throughout the rest of the house, but it's also practical if you're planning on having a lot of plants but don't want your floor to get damaged by moisture.

Mood lighting Dimmable lighting is key when relaxing in your sunroom at night. While the sun might have gone down, you can sit under a canopy of greenery and enjoy your evening.

STYLING A COFFEE TABLE

I've always found the term "coffee table" to be a little bit misleading–after all, we rarely drink coffee at these tables. More often, we gather around them with those we love to chat about our lives, watch favorite shows or movies, and sometimes play a board game or two. The coffee table plays a significant role in our homes and deserves just as much attention as the kitchen or dining table. So when it comes to styling yours, you'll want it to stand out while also providing a space to display those decorative pieces that make your room feel polished and inviting.

» Firstly, remove everything that's on the coffee table, so you can see it with fresh eyes. This is also a good opportunity to wipe the table down before you begin.

» The items you choose to style on the table should relate not only to the size, color, and texture of the table, but also the overall design and aesthetic of the room. For instance, if your coffee table is white, the items that you style on top should be a bright color, to stand out from the table. If you're working with a small surface, you'll have to simplify your styling and do more with less. It's also important to be mindful of how the surface is utilized daily or when you have guests.

» Start by adding the statement piece of the table to create a focal point. This could be a ceramic bowl, stone sculpture, or a plant. If opting for a plant, remember to choose a species that will thrive in the available light. Once you've decided on this statement piece, place it on the side of the table with the least amount of use. This will keep it out of the way, but allow it to anchor the table.

» The next item is, of course, the perfect accessory for every coffee table—the coffee-table book. These books are typically image-rich and focus on topics such as art, design, fashion, and even plants (shout-out to all the wonderful people out there who have ever styled my books on a surface in their home!). These are not books that you'll be flipping through daily, but are placed here to reflect the mood

of the room and to give visitors a small glimpse into your tastes and interests. The size of the books will vary depending on the dimensions of the table, but this is a great opportunity to create a stack by layering multiple books in order of size, with the largest book at the bottom of the stack.

» It's time to sprinkle in the small personal touches—perhaps a small tray holding a scented candle or incense, a smaller knickknack, or treasured item. I typically select a tray that's a different material to the table. So if a coffee table is made of wood, I'd choose a stone or ceramic tray, or vice versa. Finally, I add a stack of coasters, hoping that anyone sitting around the table will use them if they are partaking in coffee

or other beverages, especially if the table has a wooden surface.

» The same tips can be applied to styling the top of a credenza (dresser), side table, nightstand, or console. Styling these surfaces brings another layer of beauty and creativity and completes the look of a room.

SECOND TIME AROUND

When we purchased our home, we knew we would need to break its renovation into two phases. Firstly, Fiona was pregnant with Holland, and we didn't want to remain in our rental apartment while waiting for a full renovation of the house to be completed. Secondly, after moving in we just didn't have the budget. The second phase of renovating took place three years after we moved into the house and included the bedroom suite on the second floor and the guest room. It also gave us the opportunity to redesign the nursery, the new toddler room, and the upstairs landing at the same time. Just so you know, this is quite normal—the less visible areas of the home usually end up being the last thing you focus on.

The suite entry

After three years of living in the house, we finally decided to tackle the renovation of our primary suite. When we purchased the property, this area of the home was already separated as its own suite of sorts, consisting of two bedrooms, one bigger than the other, with a bathroom sandwiched in between the two. The previous owners had used the larger room as their primary bedroom and the smaller bedroom as a place to store their clothing.

For our first three years in the house, we used the space just as the previous owners had, but knew that down the road we'd want to renovate the bathroom and reconfigure the smaller bedroom as an official dressing room. For this second stage of the renovation we decided to work with Victor Sanchez of The Boxwood Company as our contractor with Ariana Grieu as the architect. Fiona and I knew Victor personally, and I had briefly worked with Ariana on a project in the past. We loved the work that both had done and thought they would be perfect for our suite renovation and also the renovation of the guest room (see pages 172–185).

As with the entryway at the front of the house, the suite entry would set the tone for the look and feel of the entire suite. Well, not necessarily the "entire" suite because I wanted the primary bedroom to have its own vibe separate from that of the bathroom and dressing room, which would share the same color palette as the entry. The reason for this was because, as you climb the staircase to the second-floor landing, the first thing you see are the double doors leading into the suite. When they are open, the first room that is glimpsed is the bathroom. So in terms of design, I thought it would make more sense to have the entry feel like an extension of the bathroom and dressing room.

SIZE 39 SQ FT/3.6 SQ M
CEILING HEIGHT 7.8 FT/2.38 M
ASPECT MIDDLE OF THE HOUSE

When it came to styling the entry, given that it's a small space, there wasn't much that was needed. The goal was to make it feel attractive, even though it's simply an area to pass through. As the entry is almost a perfect square in shape, I thought a round rug would stand out and create a sense of intimacy, and chose a jute rug to add a little texture and pair well with those in the adjoining rooms. On the wall closest to our bedroom, I've hung a framed photo of Fiona and me taken at our wedding.

The thing that creates the "wow" moment when entering the suite is the wild change in color. Once those doors swing open, you are greeted with a shell-pink color that just instantly calls for your attention. These walls are limewashed, just like the walls in the dressing room, and on the ceiling is a smaller version of the brass-coloured flush-mount light we have in the dressing room.

The suite entry is just a small reflection of the bathroom and dressing room, but it adds so much to the overall feel of the full suite. In my opinion, it's what one might call a "sweet" suite. (OK, that was a little lame, might delete later...)

The primary bedroom

When you think about your ideal bedroom, what are the words that come to mind? For me, sanctuary, relaxing, warm, intimate, cozy, tranquil, secluded, and serene are the words I'd use to describe my design aesthetic when designing a bedroom. This should be a room to retreat to, a place to relax and restore energy, be intimate with a partner, or simply somewhere to take a snooze, a siesta, or get a bit of shut-eye. They say we sleep for about a third of our lifespan, so when you think about it, we spend a great deal of time within the walls of a bedroom, making it of utmost importance that you create the perfect space for yourself.

THE BLANK CANVAS

This is how the primary bedroom looked before the renovation took place (left). I recall walking in and thinking that not much needed to change, but the room definitely needed to be refreshed. I just had to figure out what to do with those small built-in closets either side of the main window.

Concept and moodboard

Every room in the home has its key pieces, and the images that would be displayed on a bedroom Bingo card are as follows: a bed, pillows, nightstands, lamps, a dresser or armoire, a rug, and a plant. These are the essential elements of a bedroom and when you're able to bring them together harmoniously, the look and feel of the space is resounding.

When approaching the decor of a room, I start by identifying what my theme or vibe will be. Think of this as trying to tell the story of the room, and that will guide you in the decisions you're making. Before purchasing pieces to furnish the room, I identify the look and feel I want to create, then gather a selection of samples that tell the story of the room's color scheme and include a blend of textures, hard surfaces, and decorative details.

In terms of color palette, to amplify a sense of coziness, my vision for the bedroom was a warm neutral space using shades of black and white. This scheme keeps the room simple and soft; it's bright

during the day and tranquil at bedtime. While the overall look is monochromatic, the artwork in the room provides that necessary punch of color. So making intentional choices when it came to picking out artwork, and identifying what colors would pop perfectly, was key.

The main textures here are a mix of tactile, luxurious fabrics like bouclé, velvet, and linen, and these are accompanied by a mix of metal, wood, and rattan. We retained the original hardwood floors and the combination of natural materials in the room interacts perfectly with the available light. While our home had large windows when we first purchased it, the new windows we had fitted allowed even more light to flood into the room and, thanks to the filtered glass, more controlled natural light. Lastly, as with every other room in our home, I wanted to add a touch of greenery. Plant life touches on each element of color, texture, and light and brings in the life that a room needs.

MY CHOSEN PALETTE

» The bedroom base paint is the same Sherwin-Williams Incredible White as the rest of the house, as I felt the white was perfect.

» The pops of color come from the decor and art— black, white, red, blue yellow, pink, and brown.

» The textures are a mix of woods, bouclé, linen fabric, glossy metal, concrete, stainless steel, velvet, plastic, and iron.

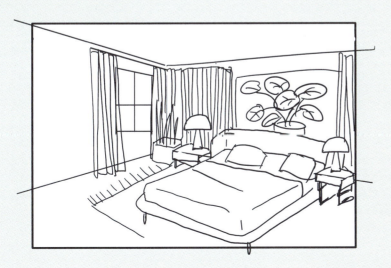

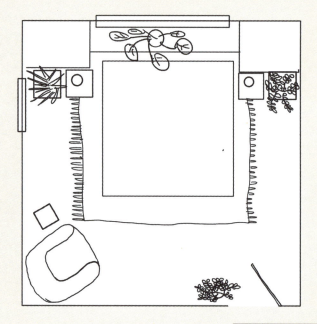

SIZE 145 SQ FT/13.5 SQ M
CEILING HEIGHT 7.8 FT/2.38 M
ASPECT NORTH- & EAST-FACING

Plan and layout

When designing our bedroom, I wanted to make sure that it not only felt comfortable and inviting at bedtime, but also during the day. The first thing I take into consideration when designing a room is the initial impression upon entering the space. Feng shui experts say it's a bad idea to have the head of the bed against the same wall as the door. The theory is that you want to be able to see the door while in bed, but you don't want to be aligned with it, as that way energy will drain out. Having the bed facing the door also creates an efficient pathway around it, making the flow of the room more practical and convenient. That said, in our bedroom I had a hurdle to overcome. Or two, to be exact.

When Fiona and I purchased our home, I could tell that the primary bedroom would be challenging to decorate. Not because it wasn't a bright, sunny, and appealing space, but due to the two corner closets that flanked the large window, plus the covered radiator between them. These large, boxy build-ins were taking up much of the room and occupying exactly the space where we wanted to place our bed. The question of how we could make the space work kept coming up.

SANCTUARY
IN SOFT TONES
The final look of the bedroom (above). I made the decision to place the bed between the two small closets and used drapes to hide them and soften the walls and corners of the room.

My initial thought was that we should simply remove the closets, but Fiona pushed back, pointing out that if we ever decided to sell the house, a closet would be necessary for that room to be considered a bedroom. Now, in my heart and mind, this house is our forever home, so I wasn't in any hurry to make decisions based on whether we might want to sell the house at some point in the distant future. Rather, I was focused on creating a primary bedroom that would bring us a sense of joy and ease while we live in the house. Removing the closets wasn't a concern for me, especially as we were planning to turn a small room next to the bedroom into a walk-in closet, removing the need for clothes storage in the room itself. But then the practical side of my brain kicked in. I knew at some point we'd likely want those closets there for storage because, as you know, you can never have enough storage. So, final decision, the closets had to stay, and I had to get creative. Sometimes it's cheaper and easier just to handle a problem with a well-thought-out solution.

DRAPED IN WARMTH

Behind the bed I styled a large *Monstera deliciosa* to create a living canopy while we sleep (above). Plants add a serene vibe to any space, and that's just what this *Monstera* is doing here. Details of the custom metal curtain rod I had made to allow me to create a wall with drapes (opposite).

Given that we wouldn't need access to the closets very often, I felt good about placing our nightstands in front of them. But once we had positioned our bed and arranged the nightstands either side, I didn't like the result. Seeing the paneled closet doors behind the nightstands looked messy and distracting, so my assignment was simple—hide the closets.

As a big advocate of making hard edges soft, I decided to hide the closets with drapery. Window coverings to be exact. I've used them in the past to cover walls, because they not only help to soften hard lines but also elevate a room by adding texture and depth, making it feel a touch upscale. I wanted to retain some of the character and charm of our home, and one detail I wanted to keep was the picture rail in each room. Here in the bedroom, I saw a way to utilize it to create a seamless look. I sketched an idea of how a curtain rod could wrap around the walls and closets and reached out to a local metal worker who was able to design and create something just right for the space.

Once the black metal curtain rod was fitted along the picture rail, it was time to cover the walls and closets with drapes. These needed to be lightweight with a clean look—the perfect counterpoint to the rod. I opted for textured crossweave curtain panels. Their soft, subtle texture added a contemporary feel and brought visual interest to the room. To match the look of the rod and to make the curtains easy to pull back when we need access to the closets, I chose black metal curtain rings with clips that simply grab onto the top of the curtain panels.

STYLE TIP

I've used drapes to cover walls in projects in the past—they can be a quick and inexpensive way to soften hard lines, as well as add texture and depth to a space. For this room, I had a local metal worker design a long metal curtain rod to run around the top of the windows and closets. The textured weave drapes hang from curtain rings with clips, meaning they can easily be taken down for washing.

COLOR BARS

Here, in this corner of the bedroom, I've created a cozy little moment for my wife and I to enjoy. The bouclé accent chair brings comfort and coolness, while the painting by artist Emma Childs provides the pops of color the room needs.

Furniture

As the statement piece, the bed is the place to start when choosing bedroom furniture—once you've picked it, all the other elements will fall into place. Sticking with my theme of indulgent and cozy, I wanted a bed that felt and looked like a big, fluffy pillow, complemented the folds of the curtains, and emphasized a sense of comfort. Being a taller human at 6ft 5in/1.95m, a king-sized bed is my ideal and, after an extensive search, I found the perfect one for the room. With its curved cotton-velvet upholstery headboard and frame, it's a beautiful modern statement that sets off the room perfectly. The color is a fleecy warm white that matches the curtains, while the black leather trim chimes with the curtain rod. Now it was time to find the right mattress.

In the past, I never put much emphasis or gave any thought to the benefits of a good night's sleep. During my adolescence and right up until my mid-thirties, sleep was not high on my list of priorities—I thought it took up valuable time that I could use to be creative and productive. I was an artist and keen to pull all-nighters, working on a painting or editing a video. The rapper Nas once wrote, "Sleep is the cousin of death," and I took those words to heart. It wasn't until I met Fiona and saw how she prioritized her sleep that I began to understand its true value. And the right mattress is the foundation for good sleep. I have tried out many mattresses throughout my lifetime but none felt quite right until we got our first Leesa mattress. Let's just say that now every mattress in our home is a Leesa.

To create the perfect stage for the bed, I placed a warm white Berber-style rug beneath it. As you'll notice while turning the pages of this book, I'm a huge fan of a Berber rug, especially in rooms where you want to create a sense of comfort. The soft, dense Berber weave encourages you to kick off your shoes and walk over it barefoot.

On either side of the bed, I placed two black-oak nightstands with natural cane drawers. The black oak pairs well with the black-framed windows, while the cane adds another texture to the room. On top, I placed two dark bronze Art Deco-style table lamps. Their sleek and stylish good looks stand out against the black oak of the nightstands but also play well with the metal of the curtain rod. I decided on metal domed lamps because they would reflect light downward onto the nightstands instead of illuminating the entire room. This way, when turned on in the evenings, they instantly create warm pools of light.

With the main characters of the room in their positions, it was time to introduce the supporting roles. First, the accent chair. Yes, the chair that ultimately exists purely to hold the clothes you take off at night and just haven't found the time to put away. Let's be honest, we start out with high hopes of sitting in this chair and reading a book while sipping a nice cup of tea or coffee, but we never get that opportunity because there is always a pile of clothes in the way. But I digress. It's the thought that counts, right? The desire for a piece of furniture that gives you another place to sit in the room. Here, I went with a warm white bouclé-covered cloud of comfort. As someone who loves the tactile softness of bouclé, it's hard for me to pass up on an accent chair covered in the material, especially when I'm creating a cozy corner. This particular chair echoes the other rounded edges that appear throughout the room, but its polished stainless-steel frame adds a nice change in materials. Next to it sits a contemporary concrete side table and behind booms out a dark bronze floor lamp. The concept of working in threes is present here, as the floor lamp links visually to the two nightstand lamps.

THE DARK SIDE

This Art Deco lamp, sitting on a black-oak nightstand, begs to be the center of attention between the bedframe and the large *Zamioculcas zamiifolia* 'Raven' (right). However, the Raven ZZ is hard to outshine when planted in one of the white square containers from my 2024 collection for Target.

Art and decor

As an artist, I'm almost offended by blank walls. Yes, I know walls are made to separate one room from another, but in my opinion, they should be utilized to display art, whether it be living or inanimate. When you hang art, give some thought to the sight lines when you enter a room. The first wall you see is the one to showcase the main piece of artwork. In our bedroom, I was looking for something with a strong pop of color but which didn't demand too much attention with its complexity or story. I wanted to utilize primary colors and a fun abstract shape and fell in love with this four-panel painting by artist and friend Emma Childs. It feels bright and dark at the same time, like a mix of day and night. I know that doesn't make sense, but that is the only way to describe the way I feel when I look at it. This piece is the standout work of art in the room, so next to it, I decided to put together a gallery wall with a mix of artworks that fitted with the color scheme of the rest of the room and also had more obvious sleep-related themes. Given that these pieces hang directly opposite the bed, I wanted them to provide inspiration for beautiful dreams or a cheerful greeting in the morning.

Green dreams

There are very few pieces of decor that have been scientifically proven to benefit you while you sleep. One that does have a health benefit is—yes, you got it—plants. Specifically, the snake plant (*Dracaena trifasciata*), which produces oxygen during the night while also taking in carbon dioxide and filtering common household pollutants. So, whenever I have the opportunity to style a bedroom, you can be certain there will be a snake plant or two thrown into the mix. Next to one nightstand, I styled a cylindrical snake plant (*Dracaena angolensis*) and on the other I placed a *Zamioculcas zamiifolia* 'Raven'. As well as its health benefits, I love the cylindrical snake because of the way its sword-like foliage burst out of the planter and fans out into the space. I chose the Raven ZZ for its dark foliage, which complements the other dark tones in the room, and its tolerance of low light levels.

With these two plants bookending the bed, I still needed a statement plant for the space, hence the large *Monstera deliciosa* that sits behind the bed. I have to be honest, the decision to place the plant here was purely based on the way it looks, and it is awkward when it comes to watering. As a plant stylist, I always make my clients aware that when you place a plant in a spot that doesn't make it easy to reach, you need to be prepared to put in extra effort to care for it. I have to climb right on top of the bed with a full can of water, then carefully reach over to water this plant. If that's not something you'll be able to commit to on a regular basis, be sure to choose a more convenient spot for your plant, because browning, curling leaves are not going to bring anyone sweet dreams.

LIVING ACCENTS
A cylindrical snake plant is the ideal counterpoint to the Raven ZZ on the other side of the room (above). Its spear-like foliage mimics the organic folds of the curtains. The large *Monstera deliciosa* is the perfect statement plant, its tropical foliage instantly transporting you to paradise (opposite).

TOP 5 PLANTS FOR THE BEDROOM

Snake plants (*Dracaena*)
Unlike your roommate, snake plants remove harmful toxins while you're sleeping. They're also slow growers and have an upright shape, making them easy to house in corners.

Monstera deliciosa
Monsteras, or Swiss cheese plants, are the perfect statement plant for the bedroom because they are a true representation of a tropical environment. When styled in your bedroom, they can transport you to your favorite tropical destination while you're snug in bed at home.

Fiddle-leaf fig (*Ficus lyrata*)
Listen, I know you don't need to have nightmares while you're asleep but having a tree in your bedroom is an instant statement and mood setter.

Place a tall fiddle-leaf fig in your bedroom and you'll never need to go camping again. You'll be glamping like the best of us.

ZZ plant (*Zamioculcas zamiifolia*)
These low-maintenance beauties grow fairly upright, so they aren't going to demand too much space in a bedroom, unlike your partner. While they would love spots in the room with lots of light, they will tolerate low-light corners and make your space come to life.

Peace lily (*Spathiphyllum wallisii*)
I hate that these plants are often labeled "office" plants. They should be known as bedroom plants because of their ability to purify the air around you while you sleep. They may be basic, but they're also beautiful.

DESIGNING A GALLERY WALL

A gallery wall is a great way to express your personal style and highlight what matters to you through a thoughtfully curated collection of artwork. For me, the goal is always to approach the design from three key perspectives: color, scale, and dimension. I like my gallery walls to tell both a color story and an emotional one—while some pieces hold sentimental value, others are just visually striking and cool to look at. At the end of the day, it's all about getting the vibe just right and, like each individual piece of art within your home, the gallery wall should make a statement of its own.

» The first step is to decide on the overall theme or story you're trying to tell with your gallery wall. Having a clear theme in mind will help you select the pieces that best fit your vision for the wall. It could be based around a particular color that ties each piece together or a subject matter. Sometimes it can be something as simple as the color or material of the frames. I also consider the tension between different pieces, and if I'm planning to add a three-dimensional piece next to a two-dimensional one. I've been known to add a hanging sculpture or mounted plants to a gallery wall.

» Next, identify the wall in your home or office where you intend to display this collection of art. Once you have chosen the area, make sure you know exactly what type of wall you're working with—whether it's plaster, drywall, brick, or concrete—since using the right hanging tools is important.

» Depending on the scale of the gallery wall I'm creating, I go about the planning in one of two ways. If the wall space is fairly small, such as in a room with standard-height walls, I find an uncluttered floor area within the home where I can lay out the artworks to get a sense of how they'll look hanging on the wall. I try to choose an area that is as close to the color of the wall as possible (you can improvize by using a sheet or cloth in the relevant color if necessary). In a room with tall ceilings, for example a room with a 20-ft/6-m ceiling, I

» With this information, I start hanging the pieces on the wall using the appropriate hanging tools. Different pieces of art may require different tools, so make sure you're set up right for this, and also bear the weight of each piece in mind.

» When all the pieces are in their place, I put back any pieces of furniture that were moved during the hanging process. Now you can step back and enjoy your own work of art.

measure each piece of artwork, then use painters' tape to transfer those measurements onto the wall. This gives me an idea of what the hang will look like without any guesswork or mistakes. When arranging the art, place the largest, most striking, or statement piece as the central or focal spot on the wall. This will anchor the whole display, making the wall feel cohesive and intentional.

» Once I have arrived at my desired setup, I measure the distance between each piece and note it down. While the spacing between each artwork may not be consistent, I like the overall wall to appear as though it's contained within a single invisible frame itself so the outside edges all align to create a square or rectangular shape.

TOP 5 WAYS TO GROW AN ART COLLECTION

As an artist, I've always enjoyed placing the art of others on my walls. But finding works that fit your aesthetic and your budget can be daunting. Here are a few ways that I've grown my art collection.

ARTISTIC FRIENDS

» I attended several art schools, so trading art with friends while I was in school was beneficial. Many of these pieces still grace the walls of my home today.

ART SCHOOL EXHIBITIONS

» Finding beautiful works of art that are budget-friendly can be as easy as visiting local art schools and colleges during their exhibitions. Buy from these and you're supporting young talented artists both financially and spiritually. I remember the confidence boost I would get as an undergrad when someone purchased my work. Shout-out to Jeanie Keys for being one of the first to do that—to this day I love her for this.

BOUTIQUE GALLERIES

» Visit local galleries and source great works there. While the prices might not always be in your budget, many galleries or platforms offer art-purchasing schemes or payment plans to make art more accessible.

THRIFT STORES AND FLEA MARKETS

» One thing that almost feels like meditation to me is visiting thrift stores and flea markets and methodically working my way through everything that they have to offer. Yes, it's time-consuming but it's how I hit my zen.

CREATE YOUR OWN

» Lastly, whenever I need a piece of art for a space I'm styling, I'll either pull one from the box of artwork I've amassed over the years or create a new one myself that's just right for the setting. Lean into your creativity and do the same thing.

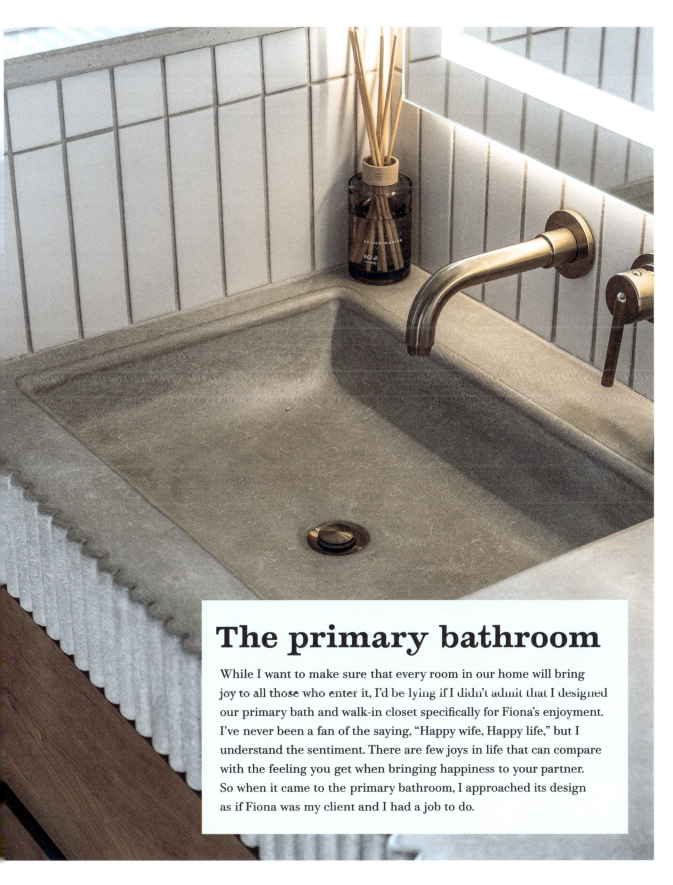

The primary bathroom

While I want to make sure that every room in our home will bring joy to all those who enter it, I'd be lying if I didn't admit that I designed our primary bath and walk-in closet specifically for Fiona's enjoyment. I've never been a fan of the saying, "Happy wife, Happy life," but I understand the sentiment. There are few joys in life that can compare with the feeling you get when bringing happiness to your partner. So when it came to the primary bathroom, I approached its design as if Fiona was my client and I had a job to do.

Concept and moodboard

When I envision a spa-like retreat I think of the five senses. I hear the sounds of running water, birdsong in a lush jungle setting, or the rhythmic hum of a tribal flute that lingers in the air like cleansing smoke. I see flickering candlelight, clouds of steam, and the sun trickling through greenery and creating dancing shadows of dappled light. Gentle, nurturing hues of orange, white, tan, and, of course, green surround me. The moisture in the air or the softness of a fresh clean towel caresses my skin. I can smell the scent of lavender, eucalyptus, or palo santo. And I can taste all of it, as I'm completely immersed in the calm and relaxing atmosphere of the space. To me, this sums up "spa-like" and it's exactly what Fiona dreamed of. I used this vision to help me recreate a spa experience in our primary bathroom.

Keeping this inspiration in mind, I started with the color scheme for the space, leaning into warm and muted hues of pink, brown, gray, cream, and green. Next, I turned to texture, picking out reeded glass, concrete, ceramic glaze tile, brass, cherry wood, cotton, and plant foliage. And, finally, I considered the light, both natural and artificial, as this dictates the mood of any space. As I've already mentioned, our home has great bones, but in this bathroom we needed to tweak the layout to meet our decorative vision and practical requirements. I sketched a plan of our desired layout for our architect and contractor, and the fun began.

While there are a few things I need in a bathroom (i.e. a showerhead that is fixed high enough for someone tall like myself), I'm generally easy to please. Fiona, on the other hand, envisioned our bathroom as a special, indulgent, spa-like retreat. And when it came to meeting this vision, we had a lot of work to do. There were many things that did not work with the bathroom we inherited when we purchased the house. I don't want to throw shade on the previous owners, but the design of the bathroom didn't feel comfortable or functional. The toilet was in the wrong spot, squeezed under the window, the shower was awkward to access, the showerhead was too low, and the vanity was just, well, wrong. Somehow, the flow felt unbalanced.

Ok, rewind. I take it all back. Actually, I do want a bathroom to change my life. As I've gotten older, I've started to realize the importance of self-care, whether that's physical, spiritual, or mental. So Fiona's hopes for the bathroom aligned with mine. Our vision was a primary bath that felt like our own private spa area. Not a simple task, but one I needed to accomplish.

THE BLANK CANVAS

Here's a peek at the bathroom prior to renovation (above left). While the layout wasn't what we desired, we were able to utilize it for three years before renovating.At first glance, the room appears to be a bit snug, but each piece is part of the puzzle to help this space reach its full potential.

MY CHOSEN PALETTE

» Designing a spa-like bathroom is only possible with the right colors, textures, and light.

» I used concrete for the sink, shower curb, and cubbies, reeded glass, cherry wood for the vanity and door, ivory-colored tile for the walls, warm-toned floor tiles, polished brass for the faucets (taps), drains, and other details, and humidity-loving plants

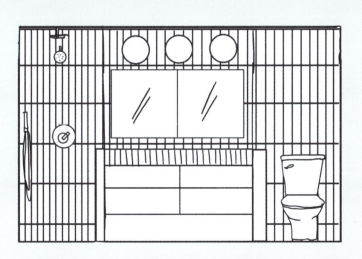

TILE BY TILE
I sketched out a floor plan, then next to that, I put together a plan for the tile layout to make it easier for the tile installer (left). The finished vanity glowing in all her beauty and warmth (opposite).

SIZE 66 SQ FT/6.13 SQ M
CEILING HEIGHT 7.8 FT/2.38 M
ASPECT EAST-FACING

Plan and layout

I started by addressing the major problem—the layout. In order to make this room somewhere we wanted to spend time, we needed to create the right flow. Most full bathrooms have three distinct zones: toilet, vanity, and shower/tub, but in the original layout, these zones were right on top of each other, making the room feel crowded yet empty at the same time. It's hard to imagine, but believe me, that's how we felt. The simple fix? Clearly define the zones. As you enter the room from the suite's entrance, my plan positioned the toilet in the first zone, followed by the vanity, and lastly, by the window, the shower. To make it even more defined, I designed half-height glass partition walls to separate each zone. I picked out reeded glass for these—not only is it gorgeous, but it also allows a lot of light to pass through it, while the view of what's directly behind is blurred.

Next I addressed the design—the look and feel of the room. I began by selecting the tile. I've always been fond of bathrooms that are fully covered in tile and knew that was the look I wanted. I also wanted to create a sense of connection with the decor of the first floor, so on the floor I decided to use the same geometric Hexite tile from Fireclay Tile that we have in the sunroom. However, upstairs I added a few more warm tones to fall in line with my color palette for the primary bathroom and dressing room and create a sense of a seamless transition as we move from the bathroom to the dressing room.

With the floor tile figured out, the next decision was the walls. Drawing on the style of our kitchen, I leaned heavily into Japanese influences here, with a simple rectangular wall tile, but relied on similar material and color combinations to the kitchen to bring the room together.

To create a better flow when entering and exiting the bathroom into the dressing room and vice versa, we decided to knock through a doorway in the shared wall. Since I had asked woodworker Andy Karnes to create the vanity, it made sense to ask him to also make the door between the two spaces as well as other wood features in these rooms. As we'd chosen red oak for most of the wood features on the first floor, we decided that cherry wood would make a nice change in the suite, as its reddish-brown hue adds warmth. We wanted

a door between the two rooms for privacy, but instead of solid wood, I asked Andy to create one with a reeded glass panel—there's something special about how reeded glass filters the light. The existing door into the bathroom was painted pale pink and Andy fitted a cherry wood trim to match the new door. I wanted the ceiling to look like Venetian plaster, so our architect, Ariana, suggested a water-resistant micro cement/concrete mix. It looks like plaster, but it's actually very fine cement that is brushed on to give the desired effect.

STYLE TIP

A spa-like experience is all about creating a sense of calm. If you're renovating your bathroom, consider putting cubbies in the shower that are not visible from the outside. There are many products you will want to have to hand, but lots of bottles can create a messy look. Having cubbies to tuck away products helps to keep the shower area tidy and organized.

Bathroom furniture

For the vanity, we asked Mark of Luke Works to craft a concrete sink with a scalloped front. This adds an interesting touch to the edge of the sink while pairing well with the verticals of the wall tile. As on the first floor, all the faucets (taps) and knobs have a brass finish. Here we used Delta faucets, and I decided to have them fitted on the wall, so we wouldn't have to deal with the grime and dirt that can build up around faucets and handles when they are surface mounted. It's a small detail, but small things make a big difference. Andy Karnes built the drawers below from the same cherry wood as the door. I specified drawers that were sleek and modern, with hidden pulls and lots of useable space inside each drawer. Mission accomplished.

Above the vanity we hung a medicine cabinet that not only had LED lights built into the mirror but also lights on the inside. The LED is dimmable and can be set to three different color temperatures, making it easy to create the perfect mood. When working with our contractor Victor and his team on the renovation of this room, I made sure to run through all the problems Fiona and I had with the current bathroom, no matter how small the issue. What bothered us about the old medicine cabinet was that when there were items of a certain height on top of the sink, like hair or skincare products, they had to be moved out of the way in order to open the cabinet doors. I made it clear that I wanted the new cabinet to sit higher above the sink. Let's be honest, the images you're seeing here show our new bathroom at its very best. It's pristine. But on a normal day Fiona, who is a busy woman, will leave products on top of the sink. That's life, right? Having the new cabinet positioned a few inches higher made a huge difference because it erased the nuisance of constantly moving products when needing to open the doors. Small fix, big result.

ATTENTION TO DETAIL

A mixture of materials makes a space feel alive (above left). Here the alabaster sconces contrast with the smoothness of the tile. They say the devil is in the detail and every detail is accounted for (above right). Here, there is vertical symmetry everywhere, which draws your eyes up and down.

With the medicine cabinet providing much of the light in the room, we only needed three small alabaster wall sconces to brighten the space and add texture against the tile. They're not there to do any heavy lifting when it comes to room illumination, but they add so much to the decor. For those times when it's necessary to fill the room with artificial light, we added two 2-in/5-cm recessed lights, one in the shower and another above the toilet (see pages 46–49 for more details on lighting).

As we relocated the toilet to the wall that separates the bathroom from our bedroom, we wanted a model with a soft flush which was also eco-friendly in terms of water use. No one needs to be woken up by water gushing through the pipes. As in the powder room, we chose a Toto toilet, and to save space, we created a little cubby within the wall for the toilet paper holder. It's easy to overlook a detail like this when renovating, but before I draw up my plans, I make sure to sit in the spaces and consider exactly how I'd like to use them. Like the vanity, the cubby was crafted out of cherry to keep everything consistent. A nice piece of art over the toilet is always recommended. Listen, as a man, I've stood in front of my fair share of blank walls while using the toilet. Adding art anywhere in the bathroom makes it feel warm and comfortable.

FINISHING TOUCHES

An image I cut out from a book by photographer Bharat Sikka and framed (top left). Our cat, Pepper, laying inside the shower to stay cool (top right). Brass accents are seen throughout my design, and these switches are the perfect blend of style and function (above left). This neat cherry wood cubby saves space for the toilet paper to hang on a sleek brass holder (above right).

Being 6 ft 5 in/1.95 m tall, it's difficult for me to shower comfortably in many bathrooms and so when designing our own bathroom, I knew the fixtures would need to be placed higher than usual. During the past few years I've traveled away from home a great deal and experienced many different bathrooms, giving me the perfect opportunity to work out exactly what I did and didn't want in my own home. The two non-negotiables were a rainfall showerhead plus a handheld showerhead, as these two things create the most relaxing shower experience. We used Delta faucets again here, in a brass finish.

While traveling, I always noted where the controls were situated in the shower to turn the water on and off. In some bathrooms they were positioned under the showerhead, so as soon as I turned them on, I'd get hit by a sheet of cold water. Definitely not the ideal scenario. Other hotels got it right by positioning the controls close to the entrance of the shower, allowing me to turn the water on without getting soaking wet and climb into the shower when the temperature was just right. OK. Place shower controls at the entrance of the shower...check! Instead of placing them on the far wall opposite the showerheads, we hid the knobs on the half-wall at the shower entrance. This way, we can avoid getting wet when turning on the water but use the far wall to hang towels. Another practical feature is the two cubbies built into the wall. While I can't control how many products find their way onto the top of the sink, at least here in the shower I can hide them away.

PRIVACY AND PEACE

Here you're seeing all the details come together at once (above). Creating a partition between the sink and toilet provided separation without compromising the space. The reeded glass divides the spaces but still lets light filter through. I designed this corner for privacy and comfort, while allowing as much space as possible to avoid that cramped feeling.

Plant life

One thing that isn't always guaranteed in a bathroom is a window. Natural light changes the way a space feels, turning a dark and depressing area into a bright and vibrant one. Natural light in a bathroom is...well, it's the dream, and we were living that. However, when we decided to change the layout, we had to replace the existing window with one that was waterproof and had a privacy filter, meaning light can flow in but no one can see in or out. This filter created the perfect diffused light for the plants that I styled in the shower. You want to make a shower feel like you're in a tropical resort? Well, just place a plant in it.

While I believe plants should be in any room that has light, one of the rooms I always style with plants is the bathroom. Since bathrooms create humidity, they provide a great home for plants such as ferns, orchids, anthuriums, bromeliads, and air plants (*Tillandsia*), which love high humidity and need frequent watering. So, if you have the proper light exposure in the shower, you'd be doing yourself a disservice not having plants in there.

Since we don't have a lot of room in the shower, I decided to hang mounted plants on the wall near the window. These include air plants, a flaming sword bromeliad (*Lutheria splendens*), a staghorn fern (*Platycerium bifurcatum*), and a *Platycerium elephantotis* fern. Not wanting to drill holes in the brand-new tile, I used Command picture hanging strips to hold them up. Yes, I know what you're thinking: "Won't that just fall right off the wall?" The answer is no, not if you do it correctly. Make sure you choose the right size Command strips for the weight of your plant when the soil/moss is wet. Fully wet, because wet soil is heavier than dry. Carefully follow the instructions for applying the strips, and

you're all good. On the floor by the entrance to the shower, I styled a lady palm (*Rhapsis excelsa*). It's the first plant you see when entering the bathroom and puts me in a good mood every time I see it.

Renovating this bathroom brought new life to our suite and added value to our home. The more time we spend in it, the more we appreciate all the thought and planning we put in to make it ours.

WILD WALLS

I added a wall of mounted plants to the shower space to make it feel more alive and spa-like (opposite above and below). I used clear Command strips to hang them so I wouldn't damage the tile. The staghorn fern happily living his best life in my shower (above).

TOP 5 PLANTS TO STYLE IN A BATHROOM

Staghorn fern (*Platycerium bifurcatum*)
Eye-catching and dramatic, when mounted on a wall, a staghorn fern makes the perfect 3D art installation. They lap up extra humidity and light, so in a bathroom you may even be able to skip the misting they require when located pretty much anywhere else.

Orchids
Most orchids are tropical plants, so they just love humidity. They won't take up much space, so are perfect for a smaller bathroom, where they'll thrive best on a windowsill in bright, indirect light.

Bromeliads
These flamboyant plants come from the rainforests of South America, so they'll be happy with plenty of warmth, water, and dappled light.

Rattlesnake plant (*Goeppertia orbifolia*)
Rattlesnakes can live with low light, but they are demanding when it comes to moisture. Humidity is helpful so they love living near a shower.

Air plants (*Tillandsia*)
When it comes to growing tillandsias, it's a matter of trying to mimic the plants' natural habitat, so the more humidity the better. Grow these in a bathroom and you're setting yourself up for success. Take care when placing them near a window as direct sunlight will make them wilt and dry up.

The dressing room

Every closet I've ever had has been pretty standard. Standard in size, standard in shape, and, most revealingly, standard in expectations. I never thought much about the closet other than its use for storing my clothing or hiding a mess when I was quickly trying to tidy my room. But I can't say the same for my mother. When I was a child, I would often hear her fantasize out loud about having a large closet. Not just one where you could hang your winter coats, like those big, puffy winter coats. No, more like a closet that you could walk right into, pirouette, then walk back out. That, my friends, is what my mother would call Special, with a capital "S." Many people would just call it a walk-in closet, but in her eyes, it epitomized status and success.

As I grew older, I started to understand that my mother's desire for a big closet was not only about status but also about practicality—as you get older, you tend to accumulate more and more clothing and storing it in a way that feels easy, tidy, and efficient is everything. And that's what I wanted for my wife and me.

The thing is, we weren't just turning an existing closet into a bigger and better one. We were actually taking a 145 sq.ft/13.5 sq.m bedroom and turning it into a closet. So maybe it would be more accurate to say we were turning a bedroom into a dressing room, because it would be an understatement to call a full room a closet. As someone who has grown up and lived in small spaces for most of his life, I am well aware of how fortunate we are to be able to turn a bedroom into a dressing room. This isn't something that most individuals have the means to do, but when it's on your dream board, being able to treat yourself to that thing is what adulthood should be about. We're creating a home in which every single inch of space is used and appreciated, and here my goal was to make sure my wife Fiona loved this room.

Concept and moodboard

When planning the look and feel of our new dressing room, I was guided by the decisions I had made for the primary bathroom. As the two spaces share a door and lead one into the other, I wanted the transition between them to feel seamless. So in terms of design, this space is very much an extension of the bathroom, and as a result I decided to replicate many of the same textures—plaster, wood, brass, reeded glass—and colors—terra-cotta, pink, cream, and brown—but to tweak them slightly to give the dressing room its own personality and atmosphere. And while there will always be plants added to every room in my house, in this room I made a practical decision to limit the amount of greenery in order to maximize floor space.

THE BLANK CANVAS
How this small bedroom looked like before we transformed it into our dream dressing room (above). The sketched layout of my desired design for the room (above left and opposite).

MY CHOSEN PALETTE

» The feeling I wanted for the dressing room was cozy and warm, with a palette of muted pink, orange, gray, and brown to complement the bathroom and the suite entry.

» The material and textures that brought the room to life were cherry-wood cabinets, polished and antique brass, reeded glass, limewash, brown leather, terra-cotta, and, of course, greenery.

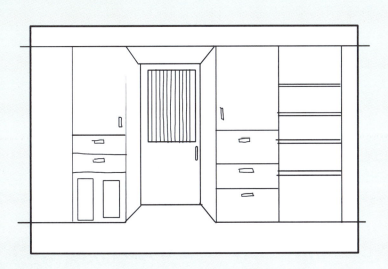

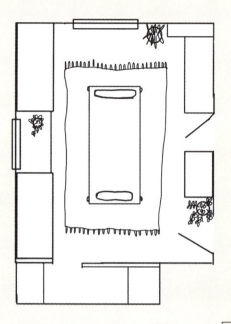

SIZE 145 SQ FT/13.5 SQ M
CEILING HEIGHT 7.8 FT/2.38 M
ASPECT NORTH- & EAST-FACING

Plan and layout

The plan was simple: to turn the room into the perfect dressing room.
And the layout was pretty simple too. The idea was to install a closet system
on both of the longer walls, giving Fiona an additional little nook that was
previously a small closet. The center of the room would be home to a nice
rug and a bench on top of that. In order to make the closet system happen,
I reached out to California Closets, known for designing and building
beautiful and practical closet/cabinet systems. Fiona and I were huge fans
of every closet we had ever seen made by them and knew they'd have the
best team to help us build our dressing room. We were connected with a
local rep and senior design consultant for California Closets by the name
of Bridgette Meushaw. Bridgette and I discussed Fiona's storage and display
needs as well as some of the features I felt would make the dressing room
work well for me.

One thing we both wanted was to be able to hide our clothes when
possible, so a system that had doors and drawers was key. It's so easy to
make a closet look like a bomb exploded in there and we knew we needed
a way to keep it organized. Fiona has plenty of long dresses, so she required
somewhere to hang those, and let's not forget space for her shoes. We

FULLY DRESSED
**The warm, muted
scheme in the dressing
room was chosen to
create a seamless
connection with the
bathroom (above).**

could have used a whole other room for Fiona's shoe collection, but somehow Bridgette made it work. I, on the other hand, had fairly simple requests. While I did get a spot for a few pairs of shoes, my priority was an ironing board built into one of the drawers. Listen, I'm a man that loves to

iron. I haven't met a T-shirt or a pair of jeans that I won't iron. Some might say, "I'm about that life!" And for those in the know, my steamer is too big for the dressing room—I keep it in another closet. Once we had shared all our practical preferences with Bridgette, I sat down with her and selected all the

I styled a leather daybed in the middle of the dressing room to give us a place to settle while getting ready (left and opposite). Adding laundry baskets to your closet keeps things efficient (above).

decorative finishes. Whether it was brass drawer handles, the cherry-wood finish of the cabinets, or the lighting inside the cabinets, these details all made the room come alive.

Once the closet system was in, I reached out to my friend and artist, Drury Bynum. Many of you will remember him from my third book, *Wild Creations*—not only did he paint the cover of that book, but he also helped to create a DIY mural as one of the projects in the book. Knowing Drury's skills at painting, I asked him to paint the dressing room walls and ceiling using a pale pink limewash. What I absolutely love about limewash is that, unlike other paints, it comes from nature, as it's made from limestone, and there's something about the hand-brushed strokes and gritty texture that I find so satisfying. I wanted the walls and ceiling here to echo what we had done in the bathroom. Since limewash does have a different texture and absorbs moisture when touched, we went with normal paint

for the doors and trim, using the same pink we had chosen for the doors in the bathroom. And just like in the bathroom, I opted for brass light switches.

Beneath one of the windows there was an old radiator that just didn't fit in with the look of the new closets. To hide it, we called on woodworker Andy Karnes to build a wooden cover that made it seem like a seamless part of the California Closets system. He used more cherry wood to craft the most elegant radiator cover. On the perpendicular wall, I placed a large, modern floor mirror, because what's a dressing room without a mirror? While its frame is made of wood, it's walnut, not cherry. There are often moments when materials and colors just don't align, for whatever reason, and here is a prime example. We've had this mirror for a long time, and I love having it where I get dressed. It has such a great look, so even though we used cherry for everything else, here we would have to make an exception. The right decision was made.

STYLE TIP

When it comes to styling a dressing room, it's a good idea to fit a large full-length mirror somewhere in the room with adequate lighting. You're going to want to be able to see your complete outfit from top to toe and get a true sense of how you're going out into the world. Large mirrors also reflect light and space, so they help to make small rooms feel bigger.

Furniture

When it came to styling the room, there wasn't much that was needed, because we wanted to make sure there was plenty of room to move around when getting dressed. For lighting, between the four recessed lights, I placed a large brass flush-mount fixture. I spotted this on CB2's website and knew I needed it for this room. It reflects light up onto the ceiling, creating the perfect wash of light, while its brass finish reflects the look of the room.

For the center of the room, I chose an orange and brown rug to complement the hues of the walls and those in the bathroom. I went with a Berber-style rug because after you spend time in the shower, there's nothing better than stepping out of the bathroom onto a soft rug. On top, I styled a brass and padded leather bench, to provide somewhere to sit when dressing. Here is where I'll find Fiona relaxing after a long shower, wrapped in a towel and taking it all in. She loves this room. I've witnessed the joy it has given my client—aka my wife—so to me, this room feels like a job well done.

WARM REFLECTIONS

The details always matter and here I've given careful thought to how each piece complements the other. This ceiling light provides warmth as well as reflection (above left). The metal and leather bench combines hard and soft materials, just as the soft Berber rug contrasts with the hardwood floor (left).

A *Dracaena trifasciata* subsp. *trifasciata* is styled in a terra-cotta pot to add to the warm tones in the room (below). I placed it in this spot because I wanted a plant that wouldn't take up too much room. As there is limited space, I'm training this satin pothos to grow up a moss pole (right).

Plants

When it came to plants, I kept it minimal, placing a snake plant (*Dracaena trifasciata*) in a terra-cotta pot at one end of the room and a low-maintenance satin pothos (*Scindapsus pictus* 'Argyraeus') clambering up a moss pole on top of the radiator cover. When styling plants in heavy traffic areas, vine plants like pothos, monsteras, and philodendrons can be encouraged to grow vertically up moss poles so they don't take up too much horizontal space. Here I made a custom moss pole from an extension curtain rod—it fits perfectly from the top of the radiator cover to the ceiling.

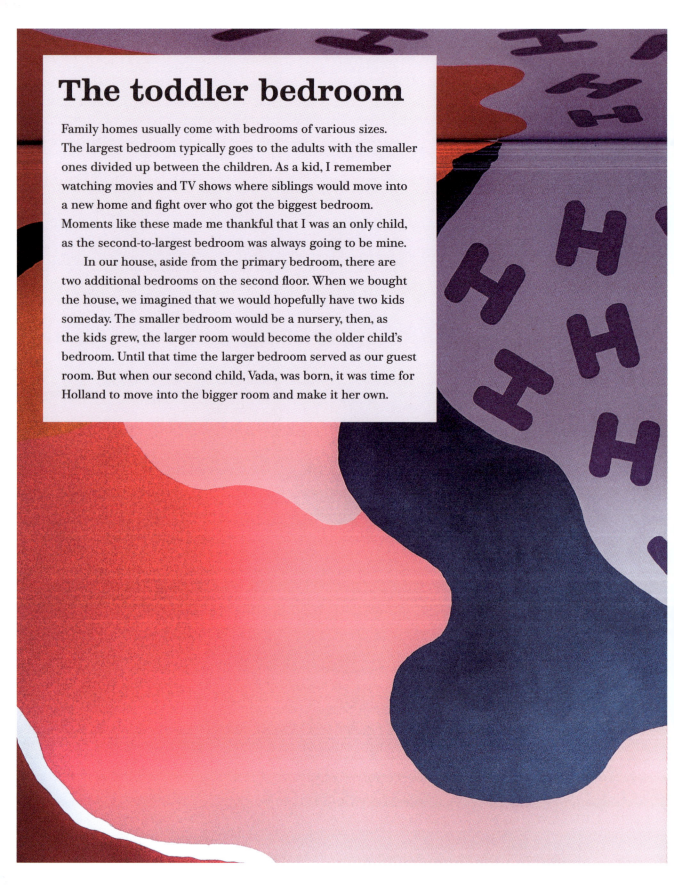

The toddler bedroom

Family homes usually come with bedrooms of various sizes. The largest bedroom typically goes to the adults with the smaller ones divided up between the children. As a kid, I remember watching movies and TV shows where siblings would move into a new home and fight over who got the biggest bedroom. Moments like these made me thankful that I was an only child, as the second-to-largest bedroom was always going to be mine.

In our house, aside from the primary bedroom, there are two additional bedrooms on the second floor. When we bought the house, we imagined that we would hopefully have two kids someday. The smaller bedroom would be a nursery, then, as the kids grew, the larger room would become the older child's bedroom. Until that time the larger bedroom served as our guest room. But when our second child, Vada, was born, it was time for Holland to move into the bigger room and make it her own.

This was the toddler room before styling. Once a guest room, the large windows made it a bright spot, inspiring me to reimagine it as a bright and playful space for a small child.

Concept and moodboard

Want to hear a funny story? Actually, I'm not sure how funny it is, but it does reveal a little about how life has a strange way of smiling at you. When we purchased the house, this room was painted purple. Now, I'm not one to judge, but purple didn't feel right for a guest room, so we painted it white. Fast-forward a few years, and guess what Holland's favorite color is? That's right—purple. Like I said, life has a way of smiling at you. So the question was, what color would she want her new room to be?

When I style a child's bedroom the intention is not to create an adult's room that feels "whimsical." Not at all. The goal is to design the space with the eyes and soul of a child in mind. Listen, my books are a judgement-free zone, but I've lost count of the number of times I've seen kids' rooms that are styled as if a sophisticated little adult sleeps in there. If it's a teenager, fine. But for an infant or toddler? Where's the imagination? Where's the sense of fun? It's like telling yourself that you'll never let your kids have brightly colored toys because they'll clash with your

carefully chosen color scheme. I've tried that and it just doesn't work. Instead, in a child's room, I focus on feeding their creative mind and soul.

When Holland was going to move into her "big-girl" room, as we like to call it, and I asked her what color she wanted me to paint it, her answer was simple: "RAINBOW!" Yes, you heard that right— not purple, but rainbow. That meant bright, vibrant, and, above all, fun. I'm the father of two little girls and, needless to say, they have me wrapped around their little fingers. If my daughter wants rainbow, I'm going to give her RAINBOW.

I don't think I need to remind you of the colors of the rainbow, but I thought adding some black and white would create a bit of contrast and bring a touch of drama to balance out all the bold colors. The furniture and decor, in contrast, would share a simple color palette with an interesting mix of textures. The goal was to create a space that had as much energy and vibrancy as Holland herself. So I came up with a plan and got to work.

MY CHOSEN PALETTE

» In this space, the mural's high energy set the tone. To balance this, I chose calming furniture and soothing textures.

» Behr Paint colors include No More Drama, 100 MPH, Gallery White, Sizzling Sunset, Blazing Bonfire, Soda Pop, Sultana, Electra, Cosmic Cobalt, I Heart Potion, and Catwalk.

» The cozy textures include bouclé, sherpa, rattan, and plant foliage.

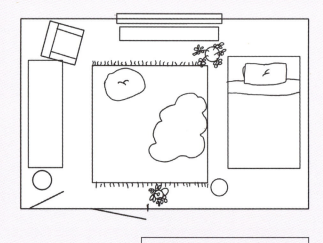

SIZE 147 SQ. FT/13.65 SQ.M
CEILING HEIGHT 9 FT 4IN/2.8M
ASPECT SOUTH-FACING

COLOR ME CRAZY

Above is my initial sketch of Holland's new toddler room, mapping out the position of the furniture. The image to the left shows a detail of the finished room painted in a rainbow of colors, just as she requested.

Plan and layout

Standing in the middle of the room, I considered all the ways I could bring Holland's dream of a rainbow-painted room to life. She didn't specify whether she wanted actual rainbows or simply a room that was all the colors of the rainbow. And given that I am an artist (or an only child— sometimes the two can get confusing), I decided to interpret it in the way I wanted, and that was as an abstraction. I decided to use all the colors of the rainbow, adding touches of black and white, and spread those colors around the room in a fun way.

I started to sketch out my ideas and allowed my pen to move loosely across the surface of the paper. Once I had finished, I realized that I wasn't painting just one wall—I wanted to paint the entire room, and not only the four walls, but also the ceiling. When I started to think further about how to make the room playful and cute, I realized I might as well paint the ceiling fan yellow too, to look like a cheerful sun.

And that's where I started, by removing the ceiling fan and spray-painting it bright yellow. While the rest of the room was painted with a flat finish, I chose a glossy paint for the ceiling fan, so it would jump out from the rest of the space. After that, I moved around the room, following the template I had drawn and getting a feel for where the shapes and colors should fall. Once the design was marked out, I painted freehand, instinctively choosing colors that complemented each other. And when I saw how well everything was coming together, I decided that I would paint the ceiling too. Listen, I love this now it's done, but I will confess that my neck and back hurt for days afterwards. It was worth it, though, as once the mural was complete, I felt such a fun, playful energy in the room.

STYLE TIP

When painting a mural in a child's room, make sure to involve them in the process in some way, whether that's choosing the color palette, helping with the concept, or even adding a few brushstrokes to the wall. Since this space is going to be their own little world, getting them involved in the creation and styling will make them feel special and more connected to the room.

Furniture

The bright colors on the walls inspired the rest of the decor in Holland's room—I could see that for anything to stand out, it would have to lean to white or neutral. And that was my starting point when it came to furniture.

Unlike with our bedroom, here it felt obvious where the furniture should go. Holland was moving from a crib to a toddler bed and we needed to choose one for her to transition into. Recalling how much she loved the tent that I sometimes set up for her in our sunroom, I thought she would enjoy sleeping in a bed that looks like a little house and found the perfect one—a cute white "cottage" bed with a trundle below. Not only would this create a space for her to sleep peacefully, but it also provided a place for a friend or—let's be more realistic—for Fiona or I to sleep over in here.

The next important piece was a dresser. I wanted something simple, clean, and elegant and found a seven-drawer one with brass knobs and a scalloped detail. It adds a sweet touch to the room and the scallops echo the scalloped design in the mural perfectly. The top of this dresser was the place for some decorative details: a small giraffe lamp, a dimmable LED "H" lamp, and a few stuffies.

Above the dresser I styled a round wooden bobble mirror. It has a playful feel, but is grown up enough to hang in Holland's room into her teenage years. The frame has a hand-painted finish that perfectly complements the walls.

THINK OUTSIDE THE BOX
Here is Holland's "big-girl" room full of all the unicorns and rainbows a kid could ask for (right). I even added little H's to the walls to make the room as playful and personal for her as possible.

INNER CHILD

A couple of Holland's stuffed animals styled neatly on her dresser instead of the floor (left). The animal-themed items of decor add a wild touch to the space, making it exciting for a small child (below). These kinds of playful pieces are easy to find nowadays, with many retailers offering fun decor for children's rooms.

When designing a room, not everything has to be brand-new—it feels even more special when treasured pieces transition from one space to another. I introduced some new pieces to add beauty and whimsy, but we kept items from Holland's nursery that were familiar and comforting, such as her rocker recliner. Fiona and I spent so many nights in this chair when Holland was an infant, reading to her, rocking her to sleep, and, of course, sleeping there ourselves. While Holland has grown older, her recliner is still a great place to cuddle up and it fits perfectly in its new room.

Knowing how much time children spend playing on the floor, I layered two rugs on the wooden floors for added coziness. The first was a neutral shag rug that covers the majority of the floor space, then I layered a white faux-fur cloud-shaped rug on top. Not only is this in keeping with the playful spirit of the room, but it also provides a comfortable spot for playing on the floor.

At one end of the rug I placed a cream shearling beanbag. This provides the perfect place for reading bedtime stories, playing snowball fights (using the beanbag as a large snowball, of course), or just snuggling. At the other end of the rug, closer to the bed, I placed a white hourglass-shaped table to act as a nightstand with a small lamp on top. Finally, on the wall beside that, I hung two white bookshelves where Holland can keep some of her favorite books.

DREAM BIG

The wall-mounted bookshelves from Pottery Barn Kids (PBK) allow Holland to choose her bedtime story each night (above right). The cottage-style bedframe also came from PBK. It feels like a fun playhouse to fall asleep in and is decorated with her favorite things, from rainbow sheets to a purple unicorn bedding set (right).

WILD IDEAS

Styling a fiddle-leaf fig and a Blue Star fern in playful baskets adds a fun, natural touch to Holland's room (left and below). Choose colorful or animal-themed baskets to make plants feel like part of the decor in a toddler room. They bring life, texture, and a bit of whimsy to the space.

Plants

I kept the plants to a minimum in this room, knowing that Holland needed space for play, not for my beloved plants. Close to the window, I placed a fiddle-leaf fig in a giraffe-shaped basket and by the door I popped a Blue Star fern (*Phlebodium aureum*) in an owl-shaped basket. Both plants are still in their nursery pots, so to make sure water doesn't drain out, I placed a base tray inside each of the baskets and underneath the plants.

When styling plants in children's rooms, it's important to be aware of the plants' properties. Nontoxic plants like air plants (*Tillandsia*), calatheas, spider plants (*Chlorophytum comosum*), and ferns are ideal. Knowing Holland and how she cares for plants, I could have styled all sorts of plants in her room. But as of right now, she's more into collecting stuffies than she is watering plants. A dad can dream though, right?

TOP 5 ESSENTIALS TO STYLE A TODDLER ROOM

Cool lighting As someone with two small kids, I know they never want to turn out the lights. So make their rooms fun and playful by adding cool and exciting lighting. This could be as simple as an animal-shaped lamp or firefly string lights.

A wild mural or wallpaper Plain, solid-colored walls can be a missed opportunity to nurture your child's imagination and reflect their love for animals, sports, or favorite characters. A mural or whimsical wallpaper sets the mood immediately and brings out the personality of your little one.

Mounted greenery Every room needs a plant and your toddler will love having a wall-mounted specimen of their own. Fun plants with animal names, like a crocodile fern (*Microsorum musifolium* 'Crocodyllus'), will spark their curiosity, encouraging them to help care for the plants.

Reading nook My girls have collected enough books to start their own little library. Why not support your toddler's love of reading by creating a cozy little space where they can curl up with a book or two. Adding a beanbag chair or a small table and chairs will bring their nook to life.

Fun diffuser Whether it's a nursery or a toddler room, adding a diffuser not only keeps the room smelling fresh but is also a great replacement for a nightlight.

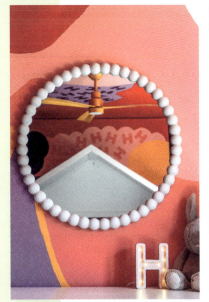

IMAGINATION STATION

A wooden bobble mirror looks like a string of beads and adds depth to the room (top left). The safari giraffe lamp brings a playful feel to the clean lines of a white dresser (top right). You can never have too many animals in a kid's room, hence the fox laundry basket, which makes doing laundry a bit more fun (below left). Lastly, a floral LED light adds all the right vibes (below right).

The nursery

When we moved into our house, I thought this small room
might become my office, but when Fiona and I discussed which
space would be ideal for a nursery, this felt the most appropriate.
With windows close to the broad canopy of a large pine tree, this
room, like the dining room, is fairly shady, making it ideal for a
sleeping infant. What also made it a perfect choice was that it
is situated on the other side of the house from our bedroom.
Now look, I'm not saying that we are trying to distance ourselves
from our daughter, but often babies wake up in the middle of
the night, and having that small distance was helpful.

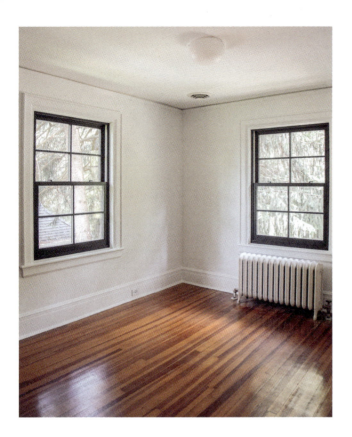

WHIMSICAL WALLS

A clean slate before styling the nursery (left). Artist Drury Bynum hand-painting the nursery mural (above). The color scheme in the mural is a mixture of a variety of muted pinks and mauves, creating a feeling of calm.

Concept and moodboard

Our older daughter Holland was the first baby to occupy this nursery. But when our second child, Vada, joined us, Holland moved to her "big-girl" room and I needed to redesign this space for Vada. I'm an only child, so was never the recipient of hand-me-down clothing, toys, or furniture, but Fiona has an older sibling and knows how it feels. She thought it would be nice to freshen up the nursery and set me the challenge of finding the right balance of old and new to make this room Vada's own.

When designing a nursery, think about calming colors that are going to encourage a baby to sleep soundly, such as pale pinks, soft grays, warm whites, muted blues, and gentle yellows. For Vada's new room, I wouldn't steer far from this color palette.

As mentioned earlier, when we renovated the house, we painted every room white to create a blank canvas. But when we decided that this room would be Holland's nursery, the plain white was quickly covered with a burgundy shade across three walls and, on the fourth wall, a hand-painted mural by artist Drury Bynum.

Knowing Drury's incredible ability to take my ideas and run wild with them, I requested a jungle-themed mural that included wonderful things that would spark imaginative thoughts in our child—unicorns, dinosaurs, and, of course, the adorable red panda. As always, Drury exceeded my expectations and created the most fabulous mural. My plan was to keep this intact for Vada to enjoy, but to brighten up the rest of the room with a fresh coat of paint in a gentle lavender gray shade called Rock Crystal. Aside from this, the existing colors and materials used in the nursery would mostly stay the same, but a few new pieces would make the space feel fresh and different for baby number two.

MY CHOSEN PALETTE

» For a warm and whimsical mood in the nursery, I used the following palette. For the paint, I went with Behr Paint Rock Crystal. Drury mixed his own blend using pink, burgundy, and white for the mural. The ceiling is Sherwin-Williams 7007 Ceiling Bright White.

» I chose warm white furniture to help the mural stand out, with some touches of brass, bouclé, and wicker throughout.

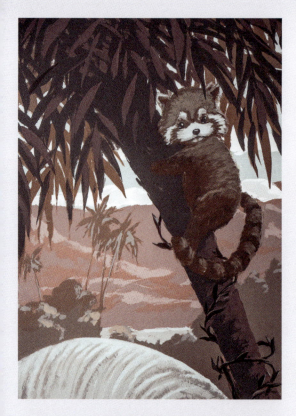

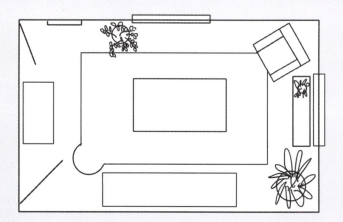

SIZE 113 SQ FT/10.5 SQ M
CEILING HEIGHT 7.8 FT/2.38 M
ASPECT NORTH- & WEST-FACING

Plan and layout

I started the makeover by removing all the furniture and decorative details, so I could get started on the painting. As I was planning to repaint the existing burgundy walls in a lighter shade, I needed to use a formulation that was a primer and paint in one and could cover the old color in one coat. This would save both time and money.

I chose the new color by identifying a pinkish-gray tone in the mural and pulling as many swatches as possible that felt close to it before settling on Rock Crystal by Behr Paint. Once I had repainted the three walls, the mood in the room instantly changed—it felt fresh and reborn. I noticed that there were a few small gaps around the mural where the original burgundy paint was still present, so I used a small brush to carefully cover them up. This helped to connect the mural and the newly painted walls in a seamless fashion.

For the floor, I chose a warm white wool rug with floral detailing. I know what you're thinking. "White rug?! In a kid's room?" I get it. But as a shoe-off household, the rug in the nursery rarely gets marked. And I knew the white would pull the crib off the floor, given the dark tone of our wood floors.

STYLE TIP

When furnishing a home, there will be times when you feel a bit bored and have the urge to bring in something new. But my goal when designing a space is to hopefully purchase "forever" pieces that can be utilized for a long period of time. Sometimes a fresh coat of paint or swapping out something as simple as drawer pulls can make a stale piece of furniture feel brand-new.

Furniture

What is a nursery without a crib? While we had a crib for Holland that did what it needed to do, Fiona and I always felt it was too big for the room, so we decided to sell it and purchase a smaller one. The new crib has a sleek modern design that perfectly fits the aesthetic of our home and the quiet feel of the nursery, and its washed pinewood finish helps brighten the room further. While a few new things made their way into the redesign, many of the pieces I originally styled for Holland stayed, such as the wooden beaded chandelier and rainbow mobile draped above the crib.

Every nursery also needs a recliner, because every parent will ultimately find themselves feeding, reading, or sleeping in the room along with their baby. As Holland's recliner was going with her to her new room, we needed to find another that was just as comfortable. After lots of research, we found the perfect swivel recliner in an ivory brushed bouclé fabric. Now, if you've read the other chapters of this book, you've probably noticed my obsession with bouclé. I love it! I'd wrap myself up in it completely if it was socially acceptable. It's so thick and soft that it feels like a hug. And what's even more special about this recliner is that it's powered, sending me parallel to the floor at the flick of a switch.

As the saying goes, "If it isn't broken, don't fix it," and that's how I felt about the mid-century-inspired six-drawer dresser opposite the crib. It still looks great as well as playing an important practical role as storage. On the other side of the room, beside the

SOFT TO THE TOUCH
A round rattan mirror reflects warmth back into the nursery, while opening up the room (opposite above). Drury's mural (opposite). Moss art, framed in colorful pom-poms, adds life to the vertical space (above right). The bouclé recliner feels like a cozy hug (right).

door, a few other pieces from Holland's nursery stayed put. I kept the white bookshelf and on top placed a few decorative items, including Vada's favorite stuffies, a diffuser, and a vase of felt flowers. Above the bookshelf I rehung the rattan framed mirror, because why would I not? The beauty of this mirror lies in the curve of the frame and the warm color of the rattan—I love how it stands out against some of the pieces in the room. When it came to hanging art and decor on the walls, I went with pieces that had a whimsical feel or added a pleasing pop of color. This is evident in the cloud-shaped mounted bookshelf, the hanging panel art that proclaims, "Come as you are," and the framed moss art that I made for Holland when she was a baby.

Plants

For a green touch, I brought in a few plants that could tolerate the low light levels in this room. Some houseplants are toxic if ingested, so it's important that any plants are either moved to somewhere out of reach or removed completely once your baby is mobile. Vada can't yet crawl, so having a ZZ plant (*Zamioculcas zamiifolia*) and *Aglaonema* 'Maria' in here, both of which are toxic to humans and pets, doesn't concern me. Once she's able to move around the room, I'll replace them with nontoxic plants like a parlor palm (*Chamaedorea elegans*) or a bird's-nest fern (*Asplenium nidus*). On top of the radiator cover, I've styled a *Stromanthe sanguinea* 'Triostar' next to a polka dot begonia (*Begonia maculata*).

DARLING DETAILS
A beaded chandelier provides fun and ambient lighting (top left). This mauve rainbow baby mobile blends with the colors in the mural and the other soft tones in the room (top right). A wall sconce providing a warm glow to the calm space (above left). Soft felt flowers add a pop of color and are a safe, fun way to add "greenery" to the room (above right).

TOP 5 PLANTS TO STYLE IN A NURSERY

When it comes to styling plants and a nursery, it's essential to consider those that are safe for children. While a newborn doesn't have the ability to move freely around the room by itself, a one-year-old can crawl over to a potted plant to get a taste of its foliage. So it's smart to plan ahead or, as I like to say, "plant ahead."

Staghorn fern (*Platycerium bifurcatum*)
This is the most interesting and fun plant to style—the fronds resemble the antlers of a stag and you also have the option of placing it in a pot or mounting it on the wall.

Rattlesnake plant (*Goeppertia insignis*)
These plants can tolerate low light, which makes them easy to grow. They open their leaves in the morning and close them at night, which makes them fun.

Spider plant (*Chlorophytum comosum*)
Which kid wouldn't like a plant named after an insect? The spider plant is easy to care for and even easier to propagate.

Crocodile fern
(*Microsorum musifolium* 'Crocodyllus')
I bet you're finally starting to get the picture. Plants that resemble or have the names of animals are always going to be a winner in the heart of a child.

Air plants (*Tillandsia*)
Small and cute, just like your kids.

PERFECTLY PLACED
Stromanthe sanguinea 'Triostar' and *Begonia maculata* in a bright window add life and color along the windowsill (above right). An *Aglaonema* styled in a wicker basket softens the corners and brings a pop of green (right).

The guest room

After designing and styling our guest room—and seeing how much our guests enjoy it—I'd be lying to you if I didn't admit to a few pangs of envy. I mean, come on! Vaulted ceilings, skylights, lush plants, and a whole floor away from our kids—it's paradise! Now don't get me wrong—I love the way I styled our bedroom. Since it didn't need a full renovation, I worked with what was already there, and it came out beautifully. But when it came to the guest room, it was a different story. I spent far more time planning out the design and renovation because, well, it needed it.

BEFORE AND AFTER
The attic before we renovated and turned it into a guest room (far left). The purple walls, dull beige carpet, and crumbling plaster made it a must for a makeover. The finished guest room, fully renovated (left). The before and after photos feel as different as night and day.

When we first moved in, we used this room, located on the top floor of our house, as a storage space for clothes, toys, random pieces of furniture, holiday decorations, and even my Peloton—all the usual stuff that gets stashed away in the attic. The previous owner had used it as a bedroom, and it had purple walls, beige carpet, and an air conditioner sticking out of one of the windows, so it felt dark and gloomy even in the daytime.

Originally, Fiona and I designated a room on the second floor as the guest room and so it wasn't until Fiona was pregnant with Vada that we had to consider renovating the attic. We knew that at around six months, Vada would move into the nursery, which meant Holland would transition into the former guest room. However, there were many issues to resolve before we felt comfortable having guests sleep in this space.

Concept and moodboard

When I envisioned the look and feel of the new guest room, I leaned into the idea of creating a space that felt like being in the center of a cloud—light and airy, and completely different from the rest of the house. I wanted to give this room the "wow" factor and the basis for that was an all-white color scheme. Walls, ceiling, and even the floors were painted a bright white to transform what was once a dull, poorly lit room into something fresh and uplifting—exactly the atmosphere I want to offer guests in our home.

With the foundation of the room being a cool, neutral white, I brought in a sense of warmth through the colors and textures of the decor, which give the room a youthful, eclectic energy. Pops of yellow, red, black, brown, green, and blue all add vibrancy, while a tactile mix of materials includes reclaimed and finished wood, metal, hemp, concrete, and plastic. The result is a room that's fun and unique with a welcoming, cozy vibe.

MY CHOSEN PALETTE

» Bright and vibrant colors set off by lots of white.

» Floor paint: Sherwin-Williams Armorseal Tread-Plex Extra White. Ceiling paint: Behr 558 Ultra Pure White. Baseboards, doors, trim: Sherwin-Williams Cashmere Extra White.

» Textures: Hemp-concrete sconces, brass switches, rattan chair, walnut tables, powder-coated steel table, bouclé/linen, plastic/terra-cotta pots, wool rugs.

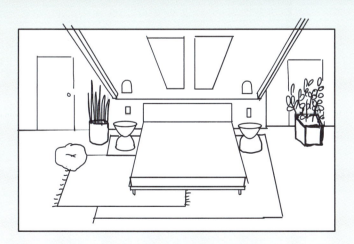

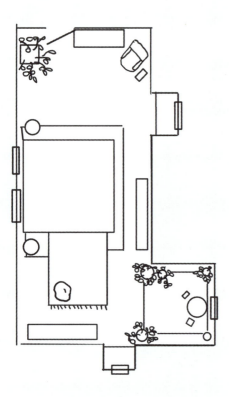

SIZE 310 SQ FT/28.8 SQ M
CEILING HEIGHT 15 FT/4.5 M
ASPECT NORTH-, EAST- & SOUTH-FACING

Plan and layout

There is something about old carpet that makes me feel a little uneasy, so this was the first thing that had to go. Plus, I was excited to see what was underneath. There was a time when carpeting over wood flooring was the in thing to do, so when you move into a period home and remove the carpet, there's a chance you'll uncover buried treasure. And we got lucky—when our contractor, Victor, and his team pulled up the carpet in this room, we were amazed to find the original wooden flooring underneath, and in great shape too.

Due to the age of the house, the top floor wasn't insulated, which made the space pretty much unbearable in the summer months. It was great for working out and breaking a sweat, but not so ideal for having your parents or in-laws sleeping over, so we knew that new floor-to-ceiling insulation was a must. As with other parts of the home, we wanted to replace the plaster with drywall, and, if possible, to create a vaulted ceiling to give the room more height. Straight after removing the carpet, Victor and his team tore out the existing plaster walls and ceiling and there, in all its beauty, was our vaulted ceiling,

Here, our once dark and dingy attic space is now fully transformed into a bright, light-filled guest room, blooming with pops of color, texture, and greenery throughout. To make the room feel inviting, the ceiling has been removed, giving the room more space to breathe, and skylights have been added to make it brighter and more airy.

with the original wooden joists still in place. I knew immediately that they would be the main feature of the new guest room—there's nothing like a bit of old-house charm along with the new.

One of the gable dormers in the room would be used for storage while another housed the new HVAC system. Fiona and I had the idea to open up one of the remaining dormers to create more space, which meant demolishing a wall and a door. When we have friends with kids stay over, the kids love to sleep in this cozy little nook on an air mattress. The dormer was at the front of the house and had a

STYLE TIP

When you have guests to stay, the first question to ask the next morning is: "How did you sleep?" And most of the time the answer will depend on the mattress you've placed in your guest room. Think about this room as if it were your own bedroom and, if possible, invest in a quality mattress. In our house, all our mattresses are from Leesa because they provide us with great sleep. Your guests deserve that too.

small air vent, which we replaced with a window after first obtaining approval from our local homeowners' association.

As these changes got underway and the drywall went up, we began to see just how different the new space was going to look. But it wasn't until the skylights were installed that I realized how incredible the space would feel. Daylight is known to improve mood and boost energy levels, so we decided to add two new VELUX skylights on the south side of the roof. My plan was to place the bed below them, so at night guests would feel as if they were sleeping beneath the stars. When a space is flooded with natural light, it seems so much more inviting, and the skylights truly transformed this room. They allow a breeze to flow in on warm days, and during colder months, the sunlight streaming in helps warm the space.

Finally, I wanted to add interesting accents to two walls and decided that shiplap panels would do the trick. These not only break up the flat white surfaces but also complement the bold horizontal lines of the newly exposed wooden joists.

TASTEFUL TOUCHES

These brass light switches are a great touch against the white shiplap wall, accompanied by the soft green leaves of the neighboring umbrella tree (top right). These natural materials come together to make the room feel warm and alive (right). The snake plant is playing its part by helping to purify the air.

We wanted the space to feel bright and vibrant, so decided to paint the walls in the same white as we'd used elsewhere. But I also took a leap of faith. One thing I deliberated on over and over was whether to paint the floors white too. I even pulled Fiona to the side on the morning when the job was going to be done and asked for reassurance that we were making the right decision. But as you can see, it all worked out beautifully. The idea came from the queen of white floors, Leanne Ford. You see, Leanne invited me to stay in her guest house while I was in Pennsylvania on a book tour, and I was taken by her white-painted floors. Something about them felt so brave, but also so right. Brave because, as someone who can stare at a blemish on a white wall until it drives me absolutely nuts, painting my floors white seemed like a punishment. I noticed there was some wear and tear on Leanne's floors, but she reminded me that this just adds to the story of your home. And that's exactly it! Just like the concrete countertop or island that we had built for our new kitchen, the floor will tell stories and hold memories of the guests that have come and gone. And if it becomes a little too messy, there's nothing a fresh coat of paint can't cover, right?

I taped out the outline of a king-size bed underneath the skylights and designed the rest of the space around that. While I would typically place table lamps on each side of a bed, the slant of the ceiling made it difficult to find the right lamps to fit the space, and it occurred to me that wall sconces would be a great solution. Tapping into local talent, I reached out to Mark of Luke Works to see if he could make two concrete wall lights that would not only illuminate but also add another layer of texture to the room. As it so happened, Mark had been experimenting with mixing hemp and concrete to create pieces that were lighter than solid concrete and with an organic look, and the results are beautiful. Below the sconces, I added the same brass switches as we have in the primary suite.

A+ A-FRAME

Attics are usually A-shaped because they are the closest room to the roof. Before the renovation, this dormer was walled off and used as a storage area. We opened it up to create a nook where guests can have a coffee or catch up with emails. When friends with kids stay over, the children enjoy curling up on an air mattress in this snug little corner.

Furniture

Do you know the old saying, "Treat others as you want to be treated"? Well, that's how I approached the styling of our guest room. Staying in hotels during my book tours helped me figure out what a great guest room should contain. The first thing was the color scheme. All the bright white surfaces made the room a blank canvas that could be dressed with colorful rugs and art, plus natural materials and neutral colors to echo other rooms in the house. Next, I rolled out the rugs. I went with a yellow and off-white Berber rug layered over a large Persian rug in a mix of yellows, blues, whites, and orange. I positioned these where the bed was going to be placed, then brought in the bed.

A comfortable bed is key in a guest room, and luckily a king-size mattress fitted perfectly here. Pro tip: if you have the space, always go for a king-size in the guest room. We've had small families stay over, and in a big bed, they can all sleep comfortably. I chose a modern style with a walnut frame and an upholstered linen headboard. On each side of the bed stands a solid walnut hourglass-shaped nightstand that brings both style and texture. To give our guests somewhere to store their belongings, I placed a tall armoire next to the door of the room. The vertical lines of the rubberwood front create a nice visual push and pull against the horizontal lines of the shiplap.

Next to the armoire, I created a cozy little moment for folks to sit and relax, with a warm-toned Mindi wood and rattan lounge chair, plus a plush white cushion.

TEXTURAL TRANQUILITY

A detail of the overlapping rugs (above). The different styles create a fresh look. Every bedroom deserves a tranquil moment where you can sit and relax (right). Here a mix of woods adds warmth to the space. A well-stocked bookcase, low pouffe, and a reading light offers another cozy seating area (opposite above and below).

This chair sits low, so once you're in it, it holds you snugly. Behind the chair, leaning against the wall, is a framed Philip Guston poster I brought home from the Louisiana Museum of Modern Art in Copenhagen, and a linear walnut floor lamp for a spot of ambience. The final touch is the wooden side table, just waiting for a cup of coffee and a book.

On the far side of the room, I positioned a white oak bookcase along the wall. With the vaulted ceilings, this space needed something low-slung with adjustable shelves to make it easy to style different-sized design and art books. On top are various items that guests might enjoy, including a Bluetooth speaker, incense, a carafe of water and drinking glasses, and, of course, more lighting (see pages 46–49 for more on lighting). Nearby is a pouffe ottoman in case guests want to sit and browse the bookshelves. There are two alcove windowseats in this room, and my mother-in-law made seat cushions for them. With the addition of throw pillows, we had two reading nooks. Finally, in the newly opened dormer, a neon red café table and a couple of chairs give our guests a place for a cup of coffee or to do a little work if needed.

Plants

If you've read any of my previous books, you'll know that I can't exist in a space without plants, and having a room that is full of light makes styling them so easy. Skylights provide the perfect light levels for all indoor plants to thrive, so here I could choose them purely based on what would sit nicely in the room.

To the right of the bed, in a planter from my third Target collection that I painted yellow to pair with the rugs, I potted a *Heptapleurum actinophyllum* 'Amate'. While this needs bright light to thrive, it's fairly low-maintenance. I love the way its upright growth fills this corner without blocking traffic coming in and out of the door. To the left of the bed, I styled a large *Dracaena* 'Sayuri' in a white glazed pot. With snake plants, I typically "false plant" them, meaning I leave them in their nursery pots, then place them inside a designer planter.

On one side of the armoire, I placed a *Philodendron gloriosum* in a ceramic glazed planter. It's a vine, and its large, heart-shaped leaves cascade down toward the floor. On the other side of the room, I styled a *Monstera deliciosa* 'Thai Constellation' and a variegated *Philodendron* 'Florida Beauty'. Their foliage pops out against the white walls, adding more pattern and texture. The same could be said of the *Ficus elastica* 'Tineke' beside the window seat, styled in another of my Target planters. The 'Tineke' is an instant "wow" plant, and its lush shape helps to sell the treehouse vibe.

HELLO YELLOW
A *Heptapleurum actinophyllum* 'Amate' is styled in a square planter from my 2024 Target line, spray-painted yellow to play with the other yellows around the room (above left). A *Ficus elastica* 'Tineke' in the same planter in white (left).

TOP 5 GUEST ROOM ESSENTIALS

Steamer/iron Maybe it's just me, but I require a steamer or iron wherever I go. There have even been instances where I've traveled with an iron in my luggage. If you provide one for your guests, they'll love you for it. At least I would.

Reading materials Reading materials are a must in a guest room and I like to provide books about things I'm excited about—typically art and design.

Café table or small desk It's nice to have a place for your guests to have a little breakfast or catch up on emails while they're with you.

Water carafe and glasses Everyone gets thirsty in the middle of the night, so making sure that a drink of water is just an arm's length away is essential.

Somewhere to hang clothes Well, this one should be mandatory. I know we don't want guests overstaying their welcome but at least give them a place to store their belongings while visiting. That's an instant way to make them feel at home.

FLOOR DECOR
HOW TO SELECT AND STYLE RUGS

Picking out the perfect rug can be daunting, but the right one has the power to completely transform a space. Whenever I unroll a rug into a room, I think of the line from the movie *The Big Lebowski*: "It really tied the room together." That's the true magic of the right rug—it can add texture and softness while also helping to define and separate different areas within a room.

Rugs aren't cheap, so they represent something of an investment. I like to shop for them in person, to get a full sense of their size, design, and feel. For this reason, I start the search by visiting local stores. When it comes to shopping for a rug online (and this also applies to upholstered furniture), I always order a fabric sample or swatch if the company has them. And if they don't offer that, then they'd better have a good return policy.

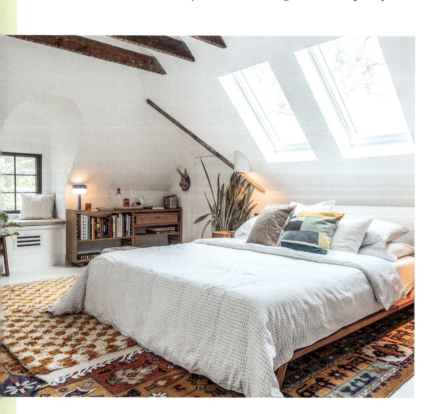

» When it comes to a rug, size matters. Getting the dimensions right is key—a rug that's too small can leave a room feeling underwhelming. So make sure to measure the space where you want to unfurl it. In a living room or sunroom, the front legs of all the furniture should sit on the rug, while in a bedroom or dining room, the rug should extend beyond the bed or table by at least 2 ft/60 cm.

» Once I have determined the size I need, I consider what style of rug would complement the room's design scheme. Rugs come in many different styles, so having a sense of what works best for your aesthetic and

lifestyle is key. I'm a Berber or shag lover myself, but only in the certain rooms. Berbers are full and soft, so bring warmth to a room and feel as if they're hugging your toes. I love a good toe hug! So I typically place them in rooms where comfort means the most: bedrooms, living rooms, sunrooms. In spaces that see a lot of footfall or high traffic, I prefer flat rugs like a Persian or modern-style rug. Since their weave is tight and flat, they aren't a trip hazard, making them a good choice for entryways, hallways, kitchens, and dining rooms.

» Now that you've identified the room the rug will go in, worked out the appropriate size, and selected a style that suits the space, the final elements to consider are the color and pattern. You don't want to team busy wallpaper with a rug with a busy pattern, as this feels too chaotic. So if the walls have a bold pattern, opt for a solid or more simply patterned rug, and vice versa. This is how I treated the rug in my toddler's room. With the colorful mural on the walls and ceiling, I opted for a neutral-colored rug to give the room balance (see pages 151 and 156–157). In some

situations it makes sense to layer rugs of different styles, colors, or textures, adding a casual and unexpected touch to the space.

» There's no need to rush the process or settle for just any rug—as I've said, choosing the right one can make a big

difference to the look and feel of a room. Take your time exploring all the different options out there and make sure the rug you choose truly complements your space in terms of style, size, and function. Because at the end of the day, the perfect rug really can tie a room together.

The Studio

I've recently been spending time getting the energy
in my new studio just right. It's definitely a work in
progress, but that's what makes it fun. All work, all
play. It is so important to establish the right energy in
the place where you create. And for me, the idea that
creativity thrives in spaces that are alive is very true.
I'm sure you will have noticed this in my previous
books—when we fill our environments with things that
inspire, like the fronds of a palm, dappled light dancing
on walls through linen shades, the texture of aged wood
flooring or sleek modern furniture nestled between
organic forms, we're not just decorating, we're cultivating.
A well-loved, intentionally designed space becomes
fertile ground for ideas. It nurtures our childlike
imagination, reminds us of who we truly are, and gives
our thoughts room to stretch, root, and grow. Just as
a plant needs the right conditions to thrive, so do we.
This is one of the key reasons I believe biophilic design
is now so popular and widely adopted by architects and
designers around the globe. Designing workspaces that
allow the natural world to creep in also opens our minds
to fresh ideas and new possibilities.

Concept and moodboard

When I have so much light in a space, you can be sure that I am going to bring in plants. I want my work environment to make me feel like a kid in a playground, surrounded by greenery and color. In this space, my idea of designing a living space is very much present. Since my studio is one of the few spaces in my life that I can truly call my own, it's a place where I can truly express who I am. When designing a work environment, the mood and feel of the space should inspire you to focus on your work, so it's important to make it yours.

The color palette that I wanted to bring into the studio is bright and vibrant with a mix of neutral tones. Colors like neon orange, yellow, red, and blue pull your eyes around the room, while a mix of neutral shades like warm white, brown, gray, and black settle you in. The textures of the studio are every bit as vibrant as the color palette. A mixture of warm wood grains next to glossy decor provides a visual push and pull that makes the space feel more exciting. Natural and ambient lighting bring an overall warmth and glow that set the tone of the space. With this quality of light and the lofty ceiling height, I took the opportunity to style the room with a variety of tall trees, drawing the eye upward and blurring the line between not only indoor and outdoor, but also work and play.

As someone who has spent most of their adulthood working from home, creating a motivating work space has always been about letting the light in. I need it. Natural light fills a room with warmth and energy, helping us feel more engaged in our work and boosting productivity. I've always chosen where to live based on how much natural light the space gets in order to keep my plants thriving, and now I use exactly that same process to find the right work environment.

I believe a great workspace, where possible, benefits from high ceilings, to prevent a boxed-in feel and to support a more open and creative mindset. So when I discovered this incredible workspace building close to my home, I jumped at the chance to take on one of the open studios. The high ceilings, large windows, and aged hardwood floors had me at "hello." Believe me, if there was a dating site for interior spaces, those qualities would be my perfect match. For me, there is nothing more exciting than stepping into a space like this—it's a blank canvas where I can let my imagination run wild.

THE BLANK CANVAS

This is the view that met me when I first walked into the studio (above left). The high ceilings, large windows, and hardwood floors felt so inviting, and, more importantly, inspiring. With natural light flooding in, this was my dream workspace. Standing there, I felt so motivated. This is the perfect space for me to create in.

MY CHOSEN PALETTE

» Unlike my home, my studio is all mine and I had full creative freedom to style it the way my heart desired.

» Inspired by the warmth of the room, I added to that by bringing in vibrant pops of color from the decor and artwork, while mixing in the lushness of greenery.

» This meant colors like neon orange, pink, electric blue, red, brown, various greens, white, and black. A full palette indeed.

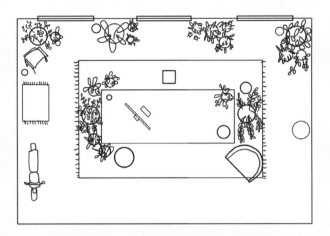

SIZE 1056 SQ FT/98 SQ M
CEILING HEIGHT 15 FT/4.5 M
ASPECT SOUTH-FACING

Plan and layout

If I had to describe the theme of my studio, I'd say it's a version of the dream that young Hilton had of a picturesque and cool artist's loft in New York City. You know, the ones in the movies where the talented but struggling artist walks into a warehouse and takes a freight elevator up a few flights, then walks out right into their studio? Yeah, that's the one. As a young artist, that was the dream. This studio didn't have an elevator opening directly into it, but it did have a similar vibe to those that I had dreamed of. What I needed to do now was to style it in a way that would reflect the dream of young Hilton, yet be functional for old Hilton.

Walking into the space, the first thing you see are the incredibly large windows. Lucky me—not only did I find a studio with huge windows, but they are also south-facing and, directly outside those windows, across from the studio, is a large park lush with beautiful mature trees. So the first thing I needed to decide was the direction my workstation should face. Have you ever been asked a question

like: "Would you rather live in a big fancy house that looked out onto a dilapidated neighborhood, or vice versa?" That's the kind of decision I had to reach when it came to situating my workstation. Would I prefer to sit with my back to the windows and the glorious view and look into the studio, or with my back to the door looking at and out of the windows into nature? As someone that adheres to the design rule that you should never have your back facing the entrance to a room, I decided it would be better to position my workstation close to the windows, which would allow me to sit with my back to them and face into the studio while I work. Once that was decided, it was time for me to style the space in a way that would make the view of the studio every bit as serene as staring out over that beautiful park. And the quickest and simplest way to achieve that would be to bring in plants.

You know how certain plants are labeled "office plants," implying that they are boring or basic? Well, I've never seen those plants that way because what's "basic" about all the different snake plants in the world? It's not the snake plants that are boring or basic—it's the workspaces that they've been styled in. When it came to styling the plants in my studio, I knew that, regardless of the type of plant, each would elevate the space and bring that "wow" factor. First, I introduced the four large trees: a *Ficus elastica* 'Burgundy', an olive tree (*Olea europaea)*, a spindle palm (*Hyophorbe verschaffeltii*), and a weeping fig (*Ficus benjamina)*. While I wasn't initially sure where I was going to position them, I knew these plants, with their height and shape, would be the stars of the show.

GREEN STUDIES

The plants in the studio bask in the southern light pouring into the studio (above). With the Hunter Douglas shades I can control the amount of light entering the space and adjust the mood simply by closing them just a bit. The calamansi tree that once lived in my home has found the right light to thrive here in the studio (left).

STYLE TIP

One thing that is of the utmost importance when styling your workspace is making sure it truly reflects who you are. Ask yourself what brings you joy and inspiration, then incorporate those items throughout the room. One thing that will have a huge impact is the type of lighting you add to the space. Thoughtfully layering different light sources helps create a warm, inviting glow that encourages focus and productivity.

Workflow

With the statement plants sorted, the next piece I brought in was a custom work table created by Andy Karnes of Area Fabrications (see more of Andy's work on pages 133 and 146). I often stand when I'm working, so I told Andy I needed a table that was taller than the average desk because I'm taller than the average man. I also wanted it to be wide enough to hold all the plants I planned to display around it, as well as those I would repot on it. I felt a warm wood would complement the hardwood floors, so I asked Andy to make the table from red oak. As always, Andy did not disappoint, crafting me a work table that I will be using for the rest of my life.

On the floor where the table would go, I placed a large 9 x 12-ft/2.75 x 3.65-m Berber rug from our local rug retailer, Carpetbeggars Hand Knotted Rugs. OK, I know I said the large plants would bring the "wow" factor, but now I want to take that back because it's actually the rug. Its bright colors and fun pattern just pop when you walk into the studio.

With the rug down and the work table in place, I decided to place the spindle palm to the right of the table and the weeping fig on the left. This styling worked for two reasons. Firstly because they were much taller than the olive and rubber trees, so if I placed them in front of the windows they'd receive much more light than the olive and rubber. And, secondly, because the spindle palm is one of the plants that I move outside to the front of my home in spring and summer and back into the studio for fall and winter, I thought it would be easier to have it sited somewhere it wouldn't get used to enjoying too much direct sun before being moved to the shadier side of my home.

On top of my work table I placed my computer (green, of course), a table lamp, a staghorn fern (*Platycerium bifurcatum*), incense, and candles. On the bottom shelf I styled a wooden tiger-head sculpture found at a thrift store in Portland, Oregon, a few plants, and some art books, for easy inspiration.

OFFICE HOURS

Smoke from incense wafts past my staghorn fern "Buck," setting the perfect vibe (left). A few items to inspire creativity should always be within arm's reach, like these that sit on the bottom shelf of my worktable (below left). A spark of inspiration can happen at any moment, so I tend to move around the studio a lot, letting it come to me (below).

Prompted by the pops of neon orange in the rug, I got a stool in the same color to perch on when working at the table. In front of the table I placed a rattan egg chair and two rattan pouffes, because in a creative workspace you want to have the option to work wherever you feel the most comfortable that day. In addition, when I have my team or friends working in the space with me, it helps them to feel at home as well.

Next to the wall, behind the egg chair, I have my easel set up, so that I can paint whenever the mood takes me. I placed the large *Ficus elastica* beside the easel and in front of the far-right window because there is something so therapeutic and relaxing about being able to paint under the branches of a large rubber tree. Along the windows, from wall to wall, I styled an array of plants that wouldn't block too much of the amazing light coming into the room but which would also thrive. These include a pencil cactus (*Euphorbia tirucalli*), dracaenas, jade trees (*Crassula ovata*), and, of course, the large olive I mentioned earlier. Most of the plants are styled in terra-cotta pots to bring warmth to the room, while in certain spots I've chosen to style specific plants in black planters to give a little structure and contrast. The large windows mean a lot of direct sunlight flows into this space, so to control the light levels, I had Hunter Douglas shades installed on each window. This means that when I'm working at my computer in the middle of the day and the sun is shining directly on my screen, I can lower the shades to diffuse the light or even block it out completely.

COME AS YOU ARE

Wearing a T-shirt designed by artist Derrick Adams that says "Come as you are" is very fitting (opposite). I wanted a studio that gave me space to create the books and content that many of you know me for, but also to provide somewhere I could paint and draw, which has been my source of meditation and therapy since I was a kid. Here, I'm captured in front of my easel, imagining the final outcome of my painting.

TOP 5 TRICKS TO BOOST WORKPLACE PRODUCTIVITY

Natural light I know this is widely known but natural light really makes so much difference. It makes you more alert and comfortable and reduces fatigue.

Storage A cluttered space can leave you feeling lethargic and overwhelmed, making you not want to work at all. Have a good storage system, so you can get organized.

A small refrigerator Having a spot for cool refreshments is a must. Why leave your studio for drinks or a bite to eat when you can have it ready for you right there?

Plants Don't even get me started with this one. If the images of my studio don't convince you that you need to add plants to your workspace, then nothing will.

A comfortable corner Every now and then, you'll want to get away from behind your desk and set up elsewhere for motivation. Style a corner in your workspace with a comfortable accent chair, a side table, a lamp, and, once again, a plant (or two). You can thank me later.

Lastly, on the far-left wall of the room, I've created a gallery wall from pieces in my art collection and some of my own personal work. Often, if I'm designing a space with a gallery wall but don't have enough art to put one together, I simply make the art myself. For instance, I wanted a big statement piece on this wall, so I made the "Sucker For Luv" drawing that hangs here (see pages 124–127 for how to create a gallery wall). In my studio, the gallery wall will always be a work in progress because I want to be inspired by different pieces of art throughout the year. It's such a great way to add color, pattern, texture, and conversation to one part of the home that you cannot achieve from a single work of art or piece of decor.

In front of the gallery wall I've parked the vintage mini Harley Davidson handed down to me from my father. The story goes that he purchased this bike while in high school and would take my mother for rides on it. One day, she told him she was pregnant with me and he never rode it again. I can't confirm if the story is true, because my parents can't agree on the details, but I love the idea of it. I keep it parked here as a reminder of the wild things we do in our youth and to remind me of both of them.

My love for styling spaces has been thoroughly documented, but if you asked what space I had the most fun styling, I'd have to say my studio. It really does reflect all that I am creatively. It's fun, it's bright, and it's wild. I have to thank young Hilton for having this dream because old Hilton is in heaven here.

RESTORING
The daylight coming into the studio is so serene and calming that when I need to take some time to recharge, I put my body in this chair and sit for hours (opposite).

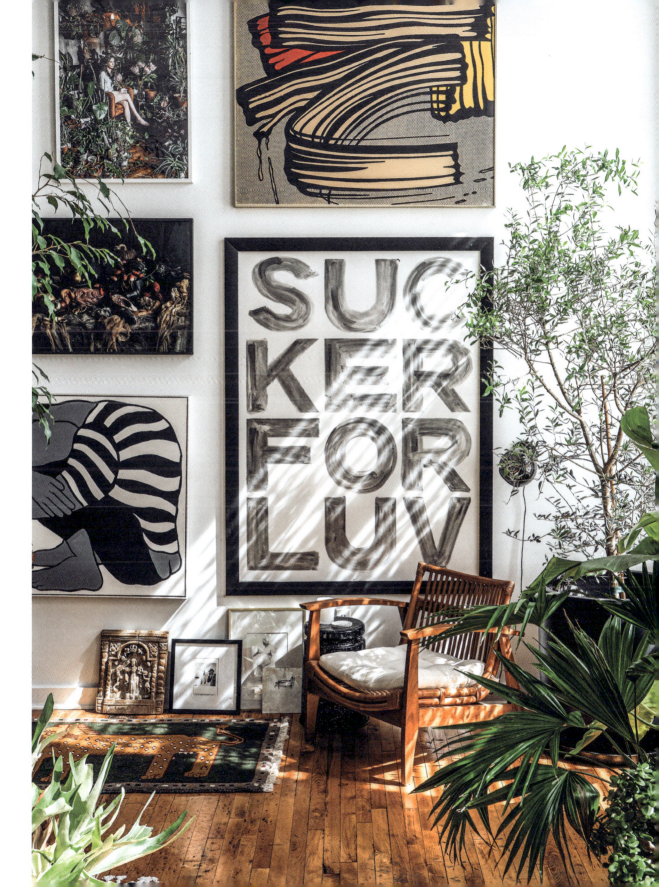

Last thoughts

After looking through the images and rereading my words on the pages of this book, I wonder whether the subtitle should have been "Designing a Home for Living." I've shared the design of my home here, but the true reason I've put so much care into each room is my deep love for my family, who live within these walls with me. Although I thought I was focused on designing a living home, in truth I've been designing a home for living.

I've chosen colors, textures, and shapes not on a whim, but to shape the mood of a room, so that those I share my life with can feel the energy, warmth, and love I've put into each space. The design choices that I've made aren't just for now but also for the future. For instance, when I chose our couch back before we had kids, I wasn't only thinking about how comfortable it would be when Fiona and I snuggled on it. I also had in mind whether it would hold up if our future toddlers used it as a trampoline or our not-even-born-yet teenagers sprawled all over it. I designed an open space between the kitchen and dining room because Fiona and I imagined ourselves cooking dinner while our children did their homework at the dining table. We added new windows on the first and third floors, so that wherever you are positioned in the house, you can enjoy views of the surrounding nature. Of course, many of the design and styling choices were made for aesthetic reasons, but only after we'd considered how they would bring life to our family.

My intention in this book is to take you, the reader, room by room through the process of designing my home, hopefully inspiring you to address the design of your own space with intention

and love. To guide you through the challenges and hiccups of a renovation. To show you that designing a space just for likes isn't going to bring you, or those who live with you, happiness. And to reveal how good interior design is, at its heart, about understanding how a space works and how the individuals moving through it live. Your home should be a reflection of you as a whole. For me, the way I work changed once I began to understand that designing a home takes place gradually and intuitively, just as the leaf of a plant or the petal of a flower unfurls in the light. That's the beauty of it all. While my home has slowly unfurled, leaf after leaf, so have I. And when you're working on your home, so will you.

If you've picked this book up hoping to get an idea of how I go about styling a room, where best to place a plant in your home, or how to design a gallery wall, you'll find all those things here. But ultimately, I hope you'll take away the inspiration to tackle your own project with enthusiasm, fresh eyes, and plentiful ideas. Remember that interior styling should be instinctive and personal, so listen to your gut. Let your space tell the story of you and those who live with you and watch as your home and your life unfurl.

Credits

All photography by Hilton Carter, except the portraits on pages 7, 188–203, and 208 by Ryan Rhodes and the exterior photograph on page 18 by Calum McKinney

Exterior Architect – Mark Mobley, Exterior and first floor renovation – Guerilla Construction
Bedroom suite and guest room renovation architect – Ariana Grieu
Bedroom suite and guest room renovation – The Boxwood Company
All windows and glass doors – Andersen Windows,

PRODUCTS IN ROOMS

ENTRYWAY
Paint from Sherman-Williams; Table a thrift-store find; Chair and lamp IKEA; Rug from Carpetbeggars Hand Knotted Rugs; Painting by Emma Childs @emmechilds

LIVING ROOM
Paint from Sherman-Williams; Rug by Chris Loves Julia x Loloi Rugs; Coffee table, bookshelf, swivel chair, and armoire from CB2; Couch from Restoration Hardware; Credenza from Thuma; Mirror and ottoman from Lulu and Georgia; Chrome lamp a thrift-store find; Sconces by Lightmaker Studio; Cat Painting by Jose Mertz @josemertz; Painting of a woman by Hilton Carter

KITCHEN
Paint from Sherman-Williams; Rug from Carpetbeggars Hand Knotted Rugs; Counter stools by Rove Concepts; Refrigerator and range BlueStar Appliances; Painting by Alina Fassakhova @alina.fassakhova

DINING ROOM
Paint from Sherman-Williams; Rug from Wayfair; Dining table by Luke Works; Dining chairs from Lulu and Georgia; Bench from West Elm; Highchair from Stokke; Cabinet from CB2; Light fixture from Horne; Painting by Jose Mertz @josemertz

POWDER ROOM
Paint from Sherman-Williams; Floor tile from Fireclay Tile; Sconce from CB2; Faucet from Phylrich; Toilet from TOTO

SUNROOM
Paint from Sherman-Williams; Floor tile from Fireclay Tile; Rug, coffee table, and lamp from CB2; Leather chairs from Dot and Bo; Bookshelf from Thuma; Wood side table from AllModern; Metal table by Hilton Carter for Target; Ceiling fan from Minka-Aire; Shades Hunter Douglas; Wall planters by Hilton Carter

SUITE ENTRY
Light fixtures from CB2; Rug from West Elm; Limewash paint from James Alexander; Light switches from Buster & Punch

PRIMARY BEDROOM
Paint from Sherman-Williams; Rug from Carpetbeggars Hand Knotted Rugs; Bed, nightstands, and chair from CB2; Floor, table lamps, and drapes from West Elm; Painting by Emma Childs @emmechilds; Ceiling fan from Minka-Aire

PRIMARY BATH
Floor and wall tile from Fireclay Tile; Faucets by Delta Faucets; Sconces from CB2; Medicine Cabinet from Illusion-B; Toilet from TOTO; Light switches from Buster & Punch

DRESSING ROOM
Closet Build by California Closets; Daybed and light fixture from CB2; Rug from Carpetbeggars Hand Knotted Rugs; Limewash paint from James Alexander; Light switches from Buster & Punch

TODDLER ROOM
Paint from Behr; all decor from Pottery Barn Kids; Ceiling fan from Minka-Aire

NURSERY
Paint from Behr; Rug, dresser, bookshelf, mirror, and chair from Pottery Barn Kids; Chandelier and sconce from West Elm; Crib by Babyletto; Mobile from ETSY

GUEST ROOM
Paint from Sherman-Williams; Rug under bed from Carpetbeggars Hand Knotted Rugs; Rug in dormer from IKEA; Armoire and floor lamp from West Elm; Bed, bookshelf, and chair from CB2; Nightstands from Walmart; Side table from Good Neighbor; Sconces by Luke Works; Bistro table and chairs from Pottery Barn; Switches from Buster & Punch

STUDIO
Worktable by Area Fabrication; Rug from Carpetbeggars Hand Knotted Rugs; Stool from Home Depot; Egg chair from Target; Lounge chair and desk lamp from CB2; Sconces by Audo Copenhagen; Rattan poufs from IKEA; Shades from Hunter Douglas

Index

Page numbers in *italics* refer to illustrations

Adams, Derrick *198*
Aglaonema 'Maria' 170, *171*
air plants 138, 139, 160, 171
Allium 'Ambassador' 23
Andersen Windows 20
appliances 60–1, 65, 200
Area Fabrications 196
armoires *39*, 40, 42, 182, 185
artworks 42, 47, 112, 136
    gallery walls 124–5, 200
    moss art *169*, 170
    murals 154, *154*, *155*, 161, 164, *164*, *168*
    top 5 ways to grow an art collection 126–7
    see also individual artists
Asplenium nidus 170
Athyrium niponicum var. *pictum* 23
Australian tree fern 45

bathrooms 108, 128–39, 142
    powder room 60, 61, 62, 80–7
Beaucarnea recurvata 45
bedrooms: guest room 172–85
    nursery 162–71
    primary bedroom 108, 110–23
    toddler bedroom 150–61
beds *112*, 114, *115*, 119, 156, *159*, 166, 182
Begonia maculata 99, 102, 170, *171*
Behr Paint 153, 165, 166, 175
benches 148, *148*
bird's-nest fern 170
Blue Star fern 160, *160*
Bluestar 60
books 104–5, 161, 185
bookshelves *38*, 40, *41*, 92–3, 102–3, *103*, 159, *159*, 170, 183
The Boxwood Company 108

bromeliads 138, 139
Buxus microphylla 'Little Missy' 22–3
Bynum, Drury 146, 164, *164*, 165

cabinets 57–61, 66, 75, 135–6
calamansi tree 62, *193*
California Closets 144, 146
candles 79, 87, 105, 196
Carpetbeggars Hand Knotted Rugs 196
CB2 83, 148
chairs 28, *29*, 182–3, 199
    accent chairs 40, 102, *118*, 120
    dining chairs 74, *75*
    recliners 159, 169, *169*
Chamaedorea elegans 170
Chanel, Coco 67
Childs, Emma 27, 28, *30*, *118*, 121
Chlorophytum comosum 160, 171
cinnamon fern 23
citrus trees *59*, 62, *63*, 64, 65
closets *112*, 114–16, 141–2, 144–5
coffee tables *35*, 40, 102, 104
color palettes 83, 108
    color pops *118*, 121
    dining room 70, 71
    dressing room 142, 143
    entryway 26, 27
    exterior 18, 19
    guest room 174, 175, 180, 182
    kitchen 52, 53
    living room 34, 35
    nursery 164, *164*, 165, 166
    primary bathroom 130, 131
    primary bedroom 112, 113
    the studio 190, 191
    sunroom 90, 91
    toddler bedroom 152, 153, 155
Command picture strips *138*, 138–9
concrete 70, 71, 180
    bathroom fixtures 84, 86, 131, 135

countertops 53, 57–8, 61
    tables *73*, 74, 120
countertops 53, 54, 57–8, 61
Crassula ovata 199
credenzas 40, *41*, 42, 105
cribs 166
crocodile fern 161, 171
cubbies 134, 136, *136*, 137
curtain rods 116, *116*, 117, 120
cylindrical snake plant 122, *122*

dancing lady orchid 99
daybed *146*, *147*
Delta 135, 137
Dicksonia antarctica 45
diffusers 161
dining room 50, 52, *52*, 68–79
doors 23, 39, *52*, 86, *86*, 92, 94, 133
Dracaena 45, 87, 199
    D. angolensis 122, *122*
    D. 'Sayuri' 184
    D. trifasciata 122, 123
    D. t. subsp. *trifasciata* 31, 64, 76, 149, *149*
drapes *115*, 116, 117
dressers 156, *158*, 161, 169
dressing room 108, 133, 140–9

entry terrace 22
entryway 24–31
Euphorbia tirucalli 199
exterior 16–23
extractor hood 60

fans 95, 103, 154
faucets (taps) 84, 86, 135
feng shui 114
ferns 138, 160
Ficus 45
    F. benjamina 193
    F. binnendijkii 'Alii' *96*, 99
    F. elastica 'Burgundy' 193, 196, 199
    F. e. 'Tineke' 184, *184*
    F. lyrata 123
fiddle-leaf fig 123, 160, *160*
Fireclay tile 84, 93, *132*
fireplace 40

flagstones 19, 22
flaming sword bromeliad 138
flooring 84, 112, *132*
    dining room 36, 70, 72
    entryway 37, 72
    kitchen 37, 57, 72
    living room 36, 37–9, 72
    sunroom 90, *90*, 93–4, 95, 103
Ford, Leanne 180
Frame TVs 40
furniture 148, 168
    bathroom 135
    bedroom 112, 118–20, 156
    dining room 74–5
    entryway 28
    guest room 182–3
    living room 40
    nursery 165, 168–70
    sunroom 102–5

gallery walls 124–5, 200
Gem, Lolo 76
Goeppertia insignis 171
    G. orbifolia 139
Grieu, Ariana 108, 133
Guerrilla Construction 22
guest room 108, 172–85
Guston, Philip 183

Harley Davidson 200
heart-leaf philodendron 45
Heptapleurum actinophyllum 'Amate' 184, *184*
Hoya 67
    H. carnosa 64
    H. linearis 87
Hunter Douglas *193*, 199
Hyophorbe verschaffeltii 23, *193*, 196

IKEA 57, 60
incense 42, 105, 183, 196, *197*

jade tree 199
Japanese maple 23
Japanese painted fern 23
juniper 23

Karnes, Andy 133, 135, 146, 196

Keys, Jeanie 126
kitchen 50–67, 72

Labisia 'Kura Kura' *99*
lady palm 45, 139
layering *36*, *78*, 79, 100,
   105
   lighting 48–9, 194
   rugs 159, 182, 187
Leesa 119, 178
lighting 23, 28, 95, 103, *170*
   bathroom 47, 130,
      135–6, 138
   bedroom 46, 48, 120,
      120–1, 161, *161*
   designing 46–9
   dimmable 48, 65, 103
   dining room 46, 75, *76*
   dressing room 148, *148*
   entryway 26, 28, 31, *31*
   guest room 179, 180, 184
   kitchen 47, 52, 65
   living room *39*, 42, 45,
      46, 48
   natural light 138, 179,
      184, 190, 200, *201*
   recessed 47, 95, 136, 148
   sconces 86, *135*, 136, *170*
   the studio 190, 194, 200,
      201
   styled light 48–9
   table lamps 120, *120–1*
   temperature 46–7
Ligularia dentata
   'Desdemona' 23
living room 32–49, 102
living walls 99, *99*, 103,
   103, *138*
Luke Works 57–8, 75, 83,
   84, 135, 179
Lulu and Georgia *42*
Lutheria splendens 138

Magnolia virginiana 18, 19
mattresses 119, 178
medicine cabinets 135–6
Melonas, Mark 57–8, 75,
   84
Mertz, Jose *41*, 42, 71, *73*,
   76
Meushaw, Bridgette 144,
   145–6
Meyer lemon tree *59*, 62,
   63, 64
Microsorum musifolium
   'Crocodyllus' 161, 171

mirrors 31, 42, 86, 146,
   147, 156, *161*, *168*, 170
Mobley, Mark 20, *23*, 135,
   180
Monstera deliciosa 23, 45,
   97, 100, *116*, 122, 123,
   123, 149
   M. d. 'Albo-Variegata' 99
   M. d. 'Thai Constellation'
      48, *96*, 99, 184
murals 154, *154*, *155*, 161,
   164, *164*, *168*

nightstands 105, 116, 120,
   159, 182
nursery 150, 162–71

olive tree (*Olea europaea*)
   193, 196, 199
orchids 138, 139
Osmunda cinnamomea 23

parlor palm 170
peace lily *123*
pencil cactus 199
Peperomia tetragona 87
Philodendron 67, 100, 149
   P. billietiae 76
   P. brandtianum 64
   P. 'Congo' 23
   P. 'Florida Beauty' 184
   P. giganteum 'Marble' 99
   P. gloriosum 184
   P. hederaceum 'Brasil'
      45, 64
   P. mayoi 99, *99*
   P. 69686 99
Phlebodium aureum 160,
   160
Phylrich 83
planters *87*, 100, *121*, 160,
   160, 199
   in-floor 62, *62*, *63*
   living walls 99, *99*, 103,
      103
plants: in the bathroom
   138
   in bedrooms 112, *116*,
      122–3, 160, 161, 170–1
   in the dining room 76–7
   in the dressing room
      149
   in the guest room 184
   in the kitchen 62–4, 67
   in the living room 45
   in the powder room 87

statement plants 23, 99,
   104, 122, 123, *123*,
   193, 196
   in the studio 190,
      192–3, 196, 200
   in the sunroom 96–101,
      102, 103, *103*
Platycerium bifurcatum
   138, 139, *139*, 171, 196,
   197
   P. elephantotis 138
polka dot begonia *99*,
   102, 170, *171*
ponytail palm 45
pothos 149
Pottery Barn Kids (PBK) *159*
powder room 60, 61, 62,
   80–7

rattlesnake plant 139, 171
reading nooks 161, 183
RH 40
Rhapis excelsa 45, 139
rubber tree *193*, *196*, *199*
Ruberto, Sarah *73*
rugs 31, 38, 40, 102, 159,
   166
   Berber-style 31, 119,
      148, *148*, 182, *183*,
      187, 196
   how to style 186–7
   jute 75, 108
   Persian 28, 182, *183*, 187

Sanchez, Victor 108, 176
satin pothos 76, 149, *149*
Scindapsus pictus
   'Argyraeus' 76, 149, *149*
shades 103, 112, 190, *193*,
   199
shelves, floating 58, 66–7
showers 130, 132, 134,
   137, 138
Sikka, Bharat *136*
sinks 58, 65, 135
slats *55*, 60, 84, 95, 102
snake plant 31, 45, *74*, 87,
   122, 123, 149, *179*,
   184, 193
sofa *38*, 40
Spathiphyllum wallisii 123
spider plant 160, 171
spindle palm 23, 193, 196
staghorn fern 138, 139,
   139, 171, 196, *197*
staircases *26*, 28, *28*

Stokke highchair *75*
storage 31, 40, 84, 200
   bedroom *112*, 114–16,
      115
   kitchen 60, 65
Stromanthe sanguinea
   'Triostar' *61*, 64, 170,
   171
the studio 188–201
suite entry 108–9
sunroom 48, *52*, 60,
   88–105
sweet bay magnolia 18, 19
Swiss cheese plant *see*
   Monstera deliciosa

table settings *78*, 79
tables *73*, 74, 185, 196
   coffee tables *35*, 40,
      102, 104
   side tables 102, 105,
      120, *120–1*, 183
Target 87, 99, *121*, 184, *184*
television 40
tiles: powder room 83, 84
   primary bathroom 132,
      132
   sunroom 90, *90*, 93–4,
      95, 103, 132
Tillandsia 138, 139, 160,
   171
toddler bedroom 150–61
toilets 82, 84, 136
Toto 136
Turner Landscaping 22

umbrella plant 45, *179*

vanity unit 84, *87*, 136
vertical planting 99, *99*,
   103, *103*, *138*

weeping fig 193
windows 19, 20–2, 54, 82,
   112
   dining room 72, 76
   entryway 26, 28, *28*, 31
   kitchen 52, 54, 58, 62
   the studio 192, 199
   sunroom 88, *90*, *93*, 94
workspaces 188–201

Zamioculcas zamiifolia
   (ZZ plant) 29, *29*, 45,
   99, *120*, 123, 170
   Z. Z. 'Raven' *121*, 122, *122*

Thanks

I am overwhelmed with joy and humility. My dream of writing an interior styling book has become a reality or, should I say, it has "unfurled" and I am just so thankful!

As always, I need to start by thanking my incredible wife Fiona, because there is no HOME without her. My love, what more can I say? I'm made more motivated, passionate, and loving because of you. Thank you. Boo Boo and Moose, you two precious angels are my entire heart, soul, and driving force. I do everything with you in mind. Before you came along, your mother and I just lived in this house, but once you arrived, we thrived. I love you.

To all my family and friends who have been so supportive through everything, from the bottom, top, and center of my heart, thank you. Thank you, my ace Ryan Rhodes for capturing my studio with your lens. You got the magic, my friend. I see you and I'm proud of everything you've become. We have much more to do, so let's keep going. To my assistant Carsen, thank you for all your help. You've become a major part of my team and I appreciate all that you do.

Thanks to Joseph Rabinowitz and the team at Guerilla Construction for starting the job of bringing our home to life and to Victor Sanchez and his team at The Boxwood Company for finishing it. The skilled work that both teams carried out has made such a huge difference to my family and me, and we will be forever thankful.

To the team at CICO Books, thank you again for the hard work you put into making our books a success. Thank you for being patient with me when it came to putting this

one together. It took a little more time than we expected but, as they say, good things are worth waiting for.

And lastly, to all of you, the designers, plant lovers, and artists, I thank you. Your continued support and appreciation inspires me to share what I love. Thank you.